THE FIRST RESPONDER ADVANTAGE

THE FIRST RESPONDER ADVANTAGE

Turn Your First Responder Skills Into a Thriving Business

Brad Newbury

Published by Game Changer Publishing

Paperback ISBN: 978-1-967424-82-5

Hardcover ISBN: 978-1-967424-83-2

Digital ISBN: 978-1-967424-84-9

GAME CHANGER PUBLISHING

www.GameChangerPublishing.com

To my family, my wife Kim, my children Colin, Bridget, and Kiera, and everyone who stood beside me through the late nights, missed dinners, firehouse shifts, and long days of building something from the ground up. Your love and support carried me through every challenge, and I could never have done this without you.

To the students who believed in our mission and gave us the honor of being part of their journey, you are the reason this work matters. To my team at NMETC, you're more than colleagues, you're family. Your grit, your heart, and your relentless commitment to our vision made this dream a reality. This book belongs to all of us.

Finally, to every first responder out there wondering if it's really possible to serve others and still build something of your own, this book is proof that you can.

Read This First

Just to say thanks for buying and reading my book,
I would like to connect with you!

Scan the QR Code Here:

THE FIRST RESPONDER ADVANTAGE

Turn Your First Responder Skills
Into a Thriving Business

BRAD NEWBURY

Foreword

We often reminisce about the day Brad sat across from us at lunch, his eyes gleaming with that familiar mix of challenge and encouragement. "So, what are you guys going to do to make this real estate business happen?" he asked, his tone steady but insistent, as if he already knew the answer was buried somewhere inside me, waiting to be unearthed. That is Brad, always pushing, always believing, always ready to guide us toward our next big leap.

For us, Brad has been more than a mentor; he's been the bedrock of our careers, the voice of wisdom in moments of doubt, and the constant force who showed us what we were capable of achieving.

In *The First Responder Advantage*, Brad distills decades of experience in emergency services and entrepreneurship into a powerful blueprint for success. This isn't just a book, it's a revelation of the unique strengths that first responders carry, a guide to transforming those skills into triumphs beyond the front lines.

For those of us who've had the privilege of learning from Brad, the lessons here are echoes of his teachings: resilience, quick thinking, and an unshakable belief in possibility. He's offered us these gifts throughout our lives, first as paramedics, then as fathers, and later as firefighters and real estate entrepreneurs, and now he extends them to you.

Our story with Brad began in paramedic school. We both had the opportunity to be part of one of the first few classes he taught. Brad didn't just train us to save lives; he taught us how to think and act under pressure, a skill that would later aid us in the unpredictable world of business.

Years later, as we stood on the brink of launching our real estate venture, we suffered a nasty case of paralysis by analysis. We had the ambition but lacked the certainty to take that first step. We analyzed deal after deal, but just kept hesitating to pull the trigger. Over another one of those memorable lunches, Brad compared our upcoming venture to a fire scene where clear, decisive action was required.

"Business is no different," he said. "You gather what you know, trust what you've learned, make a decision, and act. Sometimes it's ready, fire, aim!"

That simple, profound truth gave us the push we needed to take the next step. We made the leap, and with Brad's guidance and his knack for spotting opportunities, we bought our first building. Then another and another. Today, our success, marked by a growing portfolio we once only dreamed of, owes so much to his encouragement and practical wisdom.

For Ryan, Brad's mentorship continued at the Stoughton Fire Department. From day one, Brad encouraged Ryan to act as if he were already in the promoted roles that he aspired to achieve. He constantly took the time to offer countless pearls of wisdom like, "A good leader listens more than they speak." Advice that has shaped how he manages crews under pressure, and it followed us into our business, where collaboration has become our strength. Brad's ability to mentor Ryan in the fire service while guiding us both in real estate revealed his extraordinary range—a man who could put out the proverbial "fires" encountered in business or an actual fire at the end of a dark hallway with equal mastery.

What makes Brad exceptional is how effortlessly he bridges these worlds. The skills he honed as a first responder—adaptability, teamwork, poise under fire—are the very ones that fueled his entrepreneurial success, and ours.

In *The First Responder Advantage,* he lays out this connection with clarity and purpose, showing that the path from emergency services to business isn't just possible, it's a natural evolution. One of his favorite sayings captures it perfectly: "Pressure is a privilege." To Brad, challenges aren't burdens; they're invitations to grow. That philosophy runs through this book, a thread tying together his life's work and the lessons he's eager to share.

Brad's impact stretches far beyond us. His empathetic nature and coaching spirit have touched countless lives, both the providers he's taught and the patients they've treated. His international work, sharing expertise, driving innovation, and educating paramedics around the world through NMETC has established a new standard of excellence in our field.

To the reader, whether you're a first responder eyeing new horizons or an entrepreneur hungry for a fresh perspective, this book is a gift. Brad's wisdom will inspire you to see your own potential.

For the both of us, his mentorship has been transformative. He didn't just teach us how to act; he showed us how to do so while minimizing the downside. He saw in us what we couldn't yet see in ourselves, and with every lunch, and every lesson, he has helped transform us into the men we are today.

As you dive into *The First Responder Advantage*, we hope you feel that same spark, the sense that your skills and experiences are the foundation for something extraordinary. Brad has given us so much, and now he's giving it to you: a roadmap, a challenge, and a belief that success is yours to claim.

With gratitude and admiration,
Ryan Cabral & Jason Silva

Table of Contents

Introduction

Growing up in a small town on the Rhode Island–Massachusetts border, I found my heroes not in comic books, but on our black-and-white TV screen while watching *Emergency!* Every Saturday night, I'd watch Johnny and Roy, the LA County firefighter-paramedics, race from one crisis to another, saving lives with a mix of medical skill and raw courage. From the moment Squad 51 first rolled out of their firehouse, I was captivated. Like most kids, I dreamed of being Johnny, the charming maverick who always seemed to get the girl, but in my heart, I recognized myself in Roy: the steady hand, the voice of reason, the one who kept his partner grounded when chaos erupted.

That childhood fascination with the fire service wasn't just a phase, it was destiny calling. At sixteen, with my driver's license still warm from the DMV, I joined my town's volunteer fire department. Now, as I look back through the lens of experience, I'm amazed at the trust they placed in us teenagers. Armed with only basic training and raw enthusiasm, we were suiting up and running into burning buildings. Those early years wearing turnout gear weren't just about fighting fires; they were about forging character. The lessons I learned as a volunteer firefighter became the foundation of not just my career, but my entire approach to life.

Fast forward nearly four decades, and I've discovered something remarkable: the principles that guide first responders are the same principles that build successful businesses: discipline, quick thinking, teamwork, and dedication to service. I've applied these lessons from my years in the fire service and EMS to grow my own startup education company into a multimillion-dollar enterprise. This isn't just my story, though, it's a roadmap for you.

Whether you're a firefighter, EMS provider, or police officer, this book is your guide to leveraging your unique skills and experiences into entrepreneurial success. The qualities that make you exceptional at serving your community are the very same qualities that form the foundation of thriving businesses: problem-solving under pressure, working seamlessly in teams, and maintaining composure in chaos.

Throughout my parallel journeys in the fire service (nearly forty years) and in the business world (fifteen years), I've witnessed firsthand how the mindset of a first responder translates perfectly into entrepreneurship. The skills you've honed responding to emergencies, assessing situations rapidly, making decisive choices, and executing plans under pressure, are invaluable in the business world. This book will show you how to harness these abilities to create something that serves both your family and your future while honoring your commitment to public service.

Think about it: every shift, you face uncertain situations that require quick thinking, resource management, and effective teamwork. You've learned to stay calm when others panic, to lead when direction is needed, and to adapt when circumstances change. These aren't just emergency response skills, they're entrepreneurial superpowers waiting to be unleashed.

But I understand the challenges you face. The irregular schedules, the physical demands of the job, and the emotional toll of emergency services can make the idea of starting a business seem daunting. That's why this book offers practical, actionable strategies tailored specifically for first responders. We'll explore business opportunities that complement your current role, whether that's safety consulting, training programs, equipment sales, or innovative services you've envisioned during your time on the job.

Together, we'll work through every aspect of building your business:

- Identifying opportunities that align with your expertise
- Understanding the fundamentals of business planning and financial management
- Developing marketing strategies that leverage your professional credibility
- Building networks within and beyond the first responder community
- Managing the unique challenges of balancing entrepreneurship with shift work

Most importantly, we'll focus on creating a business that provides not just financial freedom, but also personal fulfillment. Many first responders worry that entrepreneurship means leaving their calling behind. Nothing could be further from the truth. The right business venture can enhance your service career, allowing you to make an even broader impact on your community.

As we begin this journey together, I want you to remember something: every successful business starts with a single step. Just as you once took that first step into the fire academy, EMS training or police academy, you're now taking the first step toward building your future as an entrepreneur. And just like your training officers and senior colleagues guided you then, I'm here to guide you now.

| What You'll Find in This Book

This book is designed to be a hands-on and practical guide created specifically for first responders who are ready to step into entrepreneurship. Each chapter builds upon the last, walking you through the full journey of starting, launching, and growing a business while continuing to serve in your role as a public servant. It is not a book that you read in one sitting. It is a guide to help you think about what's next for you, your future, and how you can build a business, so that you gain financial freedom for you and your family, all while serving your community.

We begin by helping you identify opportunities that are rooted in your own experience. From there, we walk through the important early decisions like choosing your business structure and forming your company. Once those pieces are in place, you'll learn how to build a solid business plan, define your brand, and communicate your message in a way that resonates with the right audience.

We will then look at the key areas that support long-term growth. You'll learn how to manage your finances, attract and retain customers, and create systems that make your business more efficient and easier to scale. You'll also find chapters on building the right team, protecting your time, and leveraging your leadership skills to drive results. Throughout the book, I've included real stories, lessons, and insights from my own journey, stories that come from years of growing a business while still working twenty-four-hour shifts in my firehouse.

Success in both emergency services and entrepreneurship comes down to *preparation* meeting *opportunity*. Your journey from first responder to entrepreneur starts now. Just as you once learned to read smoke conditions and patient presentations, you'll learn to read market conditions and business opportunities. The skills that make you an exceptional first responder are about to become your competitive advantage in the business world.

Remember: Every successful business begins with a single step. You've already proven you have the courage to run toward danger when others run away. Now it's time to channel that same courage into building something of your own.

This is not a theoretical guide. It is a working playbook filled with tools you can put into action immediately, ideas that challenge you to think differently, and strategies that have already helped other first responders find both financial freedom and personal fulfillment. You don't need to walk away from the career you love. You just need to start thinking like the entrepreneur you already have the skills to become.

Let's turn your vision into reality.

– Brad Newbury

CHAPTER 1

Igniting the Entrepreneurial Flame– a First Responder's Path

The Tones Go Off

It was 3 a.m., and in an instant, I was moving before my brain had fully caught up. Years of training and instinct took over: my body snapped into motion, the gear went on, and my mind immediately started cycling through the possibilities. Structure fire? Medical emergency? Multi-vehicle accident? Whatever it was, I knew I would be ready for what awaited us.

I've lost count of how many times that scenario has played out in my career. Every call sharpened my instincts, honed my ability to assess a situation, and refined my decision-making under pressure. The unknown didn't rattle me anymore. I had learned how to face it with clarity, purpose, and emotional stability.

But here's what I didn't realize at the time: that same readiness, that ability to shift from zero to full engagement in seconds, would be my greatest asset when I became an entrepreneur.

The Ding of the Email Wasn't a Siren, but It Might as Well Have Been

I was sitting alone in my basement home office, the house quiet, everyone else long since asleep. The soft *ding* of an email notification broke the silence. I glanced over, expecting the usual junk or low-priority messages.

But this wasn't just any email. It was from a major university. In that email, I found a contract for a strategic partnership I had been waiting for. This new relationship would fundamentally change the outlook of our business. This was the moment that could shift us from survival mode into real, sustainable growth.

My heart started pounding, not from fear, but from sheer focus. This was the moment I'd been waiting for, and now I needed to perform. The university had an expectation of delivery on what I said I could do. This feeling wasn't new. It's the same feeling I have every time the tones go off in my firehouse.

The First Responder's Advantage

Your career has equipped you with unique advantages in the business world:

- **Strategic Assessment**: Every time you size up a scene, you're using the same skills entrepreneurs use to evaluate market/business opportunities. You analyze the situation, identify risks and resources needed, and develop an action plan, all while considering multiple variables and potential outcomes.

- **Incident Command Thinking**: The ICS principles you use on scene mirror the fundamentals of what business leadership looks like: clear communication, a scalable organization, resource management, and unified command. You already understand how to coordinate resources, delegate responsibilities, and maintain control in dynamic, stressful situations.

- **Performance Under Pressure**: While others might freeze when facing business challenges, you've been conditioned to think clearly and act decisively under extreme stress. The apartment fire, the medical emergency, or armed robbery you managed last week is not so different from handling a business crisis that threatens your company's survival.

Answering a New Kind of Call

That night in my basement office wasn't about luck. It was about *preparation* meeting *opportunity*. Just like every call I'd ever responded to, I knew that when the moment came, hesitation wasn't an option. The question wasn't whether I was ready for what was to come; it was whether I was willing to do what I had learned from Chief Viscuso to "step up and lead!"

When I think about what entrepreneurship means for first responders, I see it as a new kind of calling. A new kind of mission. A new way to make a different type of impact: not about saving lives, but changing lives — yours, your team, and the people you serve in your business. I knew that, because of our school and the education we delivered, our students would make a much larger impact on patient care and future lives than any of our team could make as individuals.

You have the skillset. The mindset has already been built. Now it's just a matter of answering that next call, for yourself, your family and the people you will serve with your business.

Finding Your Why

Before we get into the mechanics of building a business, let's pause and ask what might be the most important question in this entire book: "**Why are you doing this?** What is driving you to start or grow a business while continuing to serve as a first responder?"

This isn't just a motivational exercise. It's foundational.

In his groundbreaking book *Start with Why*, Simon Sinek explains that people and organizations that understand their why, their underlying purpose or belief, are more inspired, more resilient, and ultimately more successful. He writes, *"People don't buy what you do; they buy why you do it."* That clarity of purpose becomes your North Star, keeping you focused when things get hard and guiding how you communicate your vision to others, your team, your customers, even your family.

And let me tell you, clarity around your *why* is not just helpful, it's vital in business. When money is tight, when the stress piles up, when your shift ends and you're running on fumes but still have business responsibilities waiting, your *why* is what gets you to do whatever is needed anyway. It's what gives you the stamina to keep going when it would be easier to give up.

For years, I've asked this same question in the classroom. Every time I started a new paramedic class, one of the first things I would ask my students was: "Why are you here?"

I wanted to know what was driving them toward our profession, because the road wasn't going to be easy. Paramedic school is intense. The stakes are high, the commitment is real, and unless a student has a powerful *why*, they will struggle to make it through. Some won't have the grit and perseverance needed to succeed. That's okay because, as first responders, we know how challenging our job can be on some days. You need a drive rooted in a genuine desire to serve others.

Some said they wanted to help people. Others shared deeply personal stories, such as a family member whose life had been saved by EMS or a tragic experience that had inspired them to serve. A few were seeking purpose, looking for meaning in a new chapter of their lives. Whatever the reason, when a student had a strong *why*, it always showed in their focus, grit, and ability to push through the hard days.

Business is no different. The journey of building something from scratch, while working full-time as a firefighter, EMT/paramedic, or police officer, will test you. There will be late nights, early mornings, and moments of doubt. If you haven't taken the time to understand your *why*, it's far easier to let the dream fade when obstacles show up. But if your *why* is clear, you'll keep moving forward, even when the path gets steep.

So take a moment right now to reflect on not just what kind of business you want to start but also *why* you want to start it.

Ask yourself:

- What problems have I experienced in my work that I believe I can solve?
- What impact do I want to have on my family, my community, or my industry?
- Is there a pain point I keep seeing in the field that no one else seems to be addressing?
- What makes me feel most fulfilled in my job as a first responder, and how can I bring that feeling into my business?

Your *why* doesn't have to be complicated. Maybe it's financial, you want more freedom or stability for your family. Maybe it's mission-driven, you want to create a product or service that helps others. Maybe it's personal, you're tired of working for someone else and ready to build something that's yours.

Whatever it is, **write it down, keep it close, and refer to it often.** Your *why* is your fuel, your compass, and your rally cry, especially when the journey gets hard!

And here's the good news: as a first responder, you've already *lived* this question. Every shift, every call, every time you put on the uniform, there's a deeper reason behind it. You're not just clocking in. You're showing up to serve. To lead. To make a difference.

Entrepreneurship is just another extension of that mission. But this time, you're choosing the venue. You're defining the problem. And you're building the solution.

Bridging Two Worlds

The transition from first responder to entrepreneur isn't about leaving the job you may love. It's about building bridges between them. Your experience in emergency services gives you an advantage. Here are some examples

- **Risk Assessment Mastery**: You evaluate risk versus benefit every day, a skill that translates directly to business decision-making.

- **Team Leadership**: Managing a team during an emergency response requires the same leadership qualities needed to build and motivate a business team. You already have the traits and characteristics needed, which have been honed on the street.

- **Resource Management**: Whether it's managing equipment and personnel on scene or allocating business resources, the principles remain the same.

- **Adaptability**: The ability to pivot strategies when conditions change is as valuable in business as it is on an emergency scene.

- **Network Understanding**: Your connections within the first responder community can become your initial market, your testing ground, and your source of feedback.

The Entrepreneurial Mindset

Just as you developed a first responder's mindset through education, training, and experience, becoming an entrepreneur requires developing new ways of thinking:

- **Opportunity Recognition**: Start seeing problems as potential business opportunities

- **Strategic Planning**: Think beyond the immediate situation to long-term goals and scaling possibilities

- **Market Awareness**: Understand your potential customers' needs as deeply as you understand emergency scene requirements

- **Financial Literacy**: Develop the same comfort with business metrics that you have with emergency protocols

Now that you've taken the time to uncover your *why*, the next step is just as critical: figuring out *what* you're going to build. Passion and purpose will fuel your journey, but without a solid business idea to direct that energy, it's like showing up to a scene without knowing what the emergency is. You need a clear problem to solve, a gap to fill, or an opportunity to pursue.

In the same way that you assess every emergency call—gathering information, identifying needs, and determining the best course of action—you can apply those same skills to entrepreneurship. Your experience as a first responder has already trained you to recognize patterns, anticipate needs, and take decisive action. Now it's time to take that mindset and begin identifying the opportunity that fits *you*.

In the next chapter, we'll explore how to turn your experiences, insights, and frustrations into a real business idea. You'll learn how to spot problems worth solving, determine if others care enough to pay for a solution, and begin validating whether your idea can actually take flight.

Let's get to work.

CHAPTER 2

Recognizing Opportunity—Finding the Right Business Idea as a First Responder

As a first responder, your job requires constant vigilance, quick thinking, and adaptability. You're trained to assess situations, identify risks, and make decisions in the moment. These same abilities are fundamental when it comes to entrepreneurship, especially in the early stages of finding and refining a business idea. In this chapter, we'll explore how to translate your skills and experiences into viable business opportunities and how to determine which ideas are worth pursuing.

| Tapping into Your Experiences

As a first responder, you have a unique perspective shaped by the environments you work in and the people you serve. Every emergency, every critical situation, and every moment of problem-solving has given you valuable insight into the world around you. Many of the best business ideas come from recognizing unmet needs or inefficiencies in the systems you engage with daily.

Think back to situations where you've encountered recurring problems or frustrations. Have you ever found yourself thinking, *There has to be a better way to do this?* Is there a tool, service, or solution that could make your work, or the work of your colleagues, easier, safer, or more efficient? These moments of frustration and insight are often where entrepreneurial journeys begin. By paying attention to these gaps, you may uncover a business opportunity that directly aligns with your experience as a first responder. Think about every tool you have on your truck, in your ambulance, or police car. Each one of those was designed to solve a problem, and many were designed by folks just like you.

For example, I personally identified the need for accessible online education for EMTs and paramedics. I knew there were people across the country working full-time jobs, struggling to advance their careers or wanting to care for people at a higher level, but they were limited by geography or time constraints. I also recognized gaps in EMS education availability in many regions. I figured out a way to solve that problem by creating an online platform that allowed students to receive the necessary education and training they wanted, no matter where they were in the world. The impact has been massive, not just across many parts of the US, but around the globe.

As Coach Micheal Burt often says, "Money exchanges hands when problems are solved." Every meaningful innovation, whether a tool, service, or system that improves lives, exists because someone saw a problem and stepped up to solve it. Rabbi Daniel Lapin, a respected voice on faith and finance, teaches that money is a reward, a certificate of appreciation given to those who serve others well. It is not just currency; it is a reflection of the value you create in the world. Solving real problems is not about chasing dollars, it's about building meaningful solutions that make life easier, safer, or more fulfilling. As a first responder, you already have the mindset to recognize what is not working and the instinct to act. That same mindset gives you a natural advantage in business.

Aligning Passion with Opportunity

Entrepreneurship is a long-term commitment, and success often hinges on being passionate about what you're working on. It's important to find a business idea that not only aligns with your skills but also resonates with your interests and values. Ask yourself:

- What types of problems do I enjoy solving?
- What topics or industries am I naturally drawn to?
- How can my unique experience as a first responder create value in these areas?

For example, if you're passionate about public safety, you might explore creating safety training programs for businesses, schools, or communities. If you're more interested in technology, perhaps there's an app or tool that could enhance emergency response coordination. By identifying areas that both interest you and overlap with your professional experience, you can stay motivated and engaged throughout your entrepreneurial journey.

Some may argue that passion isn't necessary to start and grow a successful business, and in some cases, they might be right. There are plenty of businesses that thrive based purely on market opportunity, financial strategy, or operational efficiency. But for me, passion has been the driving force behind everything I've built. Without a deep-rooted commitment to teaching others to "take care of people," I don't believe I could have sustained the energy, dedication, and perseverance needed to grow and sustain my business for the past fifteen years.

Building a business isn't just about strategy, it's about resilience. And when the inevitable hard times came, the grueling startup phase, the financial challenges, the moments when quitting seemed easier than pushing forward, passion was what kept me going. If I didn't truly love what I was doing, there's no way I could have worked relentless hours on my business while also pulling twenty-four-hour shifts at the firehouse.

For years, I was assigned as a lieutenant on a busy engine company, responding to calls that tested me physically, mentally, and emotionally. And yet, after those long shifts, when exhaustion set in, I still found the motivation to pour myself into building our school. Why? Because the work mattered. It wasn't just about creating a business, it was about a mission bigger than myself. That mission, that deep personal investment in what I was building, was what kept me moving forward when logic and fatigue told me to stop.

Passion may not be mandatory for business success, but I can say with certainty that it makes the journey not just possible, but worth it.

Understanding Market Needs

The next step is evaluating whether your idea addresses a real need in the market. Having a great idea is only the beginning. Successful businesses are built on solutions that customers are willing to pay for. As a first responder, you have a built-in advantage when it comes to understanding the needs of people in high-pressure situations. However, it's important to extend your thinking beyond your immediate perspective to evaluate broader market demand.

Start by asking these key questions:

- Who would benefit from your product or service?
- Is there a demand for what you're offering, or is this an entirely new concept?
- How many people or organizations are facing the problem you aim to solve?

- Are they already using another solution, and if so, what makes yours different or better?

Sometimes, you'll come across an existing solution to a problem and realize you have a way to enhance it, an approach that could outperform the original concept. I believe that truly novel ideas are rare. More often, great ideas are formed by drawing from what you've read, the education you've received, and the products and services you observe in the market. You take in that information, filter it through your unique background and experiences, and find ways to make it better. This blend of insight and innovation allows you to refine and elevate existing solutions, creating something that stands out and adds real value.

By answering these questions, you'll begin to define your target market and understand whether your idea has the potential to succeed. Keep in mind that you may need to adapt or pivot your idea based on feedback or further research into your market.

Where My Idea Came From

The truth is, I didn't invent anything new in my business. For years, colleges, universities, and private training programs have been teaching EMT and paramedic courses. Online education was also well-established in those same institutions. What hadn't been done, however, was merging online platforms with EMS education to create a comprehensive learning solution.

The idea came to me in 2005, at an EMT refresher course I was teaching. A woman approached me during a break. She knew I taught the local paramedic program and asked if there were any alternative options for attending paramedic school. I was curious, so I asked her what she meant. She explained her situation: she was divorced, raising five children alone after her husband had left and stopped paying child support. Living with her mother, she was working more than sixty hours a week to make ends meet. Despite these challenges, she was passionate about caring for others and wanted to advance her career, not only to push herself professionally but also to provide a better financial future for her children.

As I drove home that evening, her story played over and over in my mind. When I walked into the house, I found my wife, Kim, at her desk, working on an online course as she pursued her BSN at UMass Boston. It hit me: if nursing programs could effectively teach students online, why couldn't we do the same for EMS education? That was the moment the idea took root. I started thinking about how I could create a program that would enable paramedics to be taught online, bridging the gap between traditional education and the needs of those who couldn't access it through conventional means.

Validating Your Idea

Once you've identified a potential business idea, it's time to validate it. Validation means testing your idea in the real world to see if there's interest and demand before you invest significant time and money into developing it. This can be done in several ways:

Share your idea with other first responders or those working in related fields. Seek their input on whether they see value in your solution and if they would use it themselves. These conversations can provide invaluable insights, as your peers often have firsthand experience with the problems you're trying to solve.

Be prepared, though: some of your peers will be brutally honest. While their feedback might sting, it's crucial to approach it with an open mind.

Listen carefully, evaluate their opinions, and decide for yourself whether their input holds validity.

When I first shared my vision of teaching paramedics online, I encountered significant resistance from my peers. One conversation that particularly stands out was with Mark Forgues. Mark wasn't just any critic: he had been one of my paramedic preceptors, a mentor, a partner in the street, someone who had helped shape my own career in EMS. His opinion carried real weight with me. As one of the most respected educators in our region, Mark had trained countless paramedics using traditional methods, and he was convinced that online education couldn't produce the same quality of providers.

Having someone I looked up to express such strong doubts was tough. But sometimes you have to respectfully disagree with even your mentors when you believe strongly in something. Many others shared Mark's view, insisting that the traditional classroom model was the only way to train competent paramedics. But deep down, I knew they were wrong. I believed in the potential of technology and the need for accessibility in EMS education. Their skepticism didn't deter me, it fueled me.

Mark would later become one of our school's most respected educators, embracing the very teaching model he had once doubted. His journey from skeptic to advocate speaks to the power of being open to new possibilities, even when they challenge our long-held beliefs. In addition to soliciting feedback from people whose opinions you trust and respect, I'd recommend the following market research methods to clarify the situation you're contemplating entering.

Survey your target market:

- Create simple surveys to gather feedback from potential customers. Online tools and social media platforms make it easy to reach broader audiences and gather insights.

Build a prototype or minimal version:

- If possible, create a basic version of your product or service to show potential customers. This could be a simple website, a demo, or a mockup that illustrates how your idea works. Gathering feedback from real users can give you a sense of whether your concept is viable.

Validation not only helps you refine your idea, but also reduces risk by ensuring there's demand before you fully commit to launching your business.

Validating My Idea

Validating my idea was no small feat. In Massachusetts, EMS programs are tightly regulated by the Office of Emergency Medical Services (OEMS), a subdivision of the Department of Health. Getting approval for something new would be a formidable challenge. I knew I had to build out the program and prove its viability while navigating the regulations.

I reached out to Russ Johansen, the Training Coordinator at OEMS. Russ, a former military man with a sharp, practical mindset, listened as I explained my vision for an online paramedic program. He was intrigued and energized by the potential of what I was proposing. He encouraged me to map out how the program would function online and address any challenges that might arise. Most importantly, he promised to help arrange a meeting with the director of OEMS.

The next day, Russ called. The director was open to a discussion, so we scheduled one. As I rode the elevator to OEMS headquarters, a wave of nerves hit me. *What am I doing here?* I thought. Stepping into the meeting room, I quickly realized this was bigger than I had anticipated. It wasn't just the director waiting for me; the room was filled with stakeholders eager to hear my pitch.

I presented my concept, demonstrated how it would all work, and fielded a series of probing questions from the group. When the formal meeting concluded, the director invited me into his office. He looked at me thoughtfully and said he would approve a special project: one class to test the idea. I saw my chance and asked if I could run two classes for a more thorough comparison of outcomes. I knew I needed more than one class to prove the concept. He looked at me skeptically and said, "Don't push it, Newbury." But after a moment, he nodded and agreed that two cohorts would provide better data and approved my request.

That moment was the breakthrough I needed. It was proof that with the right preparation, persistence, and a clear plan, even the most regulated barriers could be overcome. It marked the beginning of turning my vision into reality and laid the foundation for a new era in EMS education.

Assessing Feasibility

Once you've identified a business idea, it's essential to assess whether it's truly feasible. This means thinking through the practical aspects of bringing your idea to life and determining whether it can succeed in the real world. Here are some key factors to consider:

- **What resources will you need to get started?** Think about the equipment, personnel, and funding required to launch your business. Do you have access to these resources, or will you need to find ways to secure them?

- **How much time can you realistically dedicate to your business?** As a first responder, your work is demanding, so it's important to assess how much time and energy you can devote to building a business alongside your current career. You should really ask yourself: What are you willing to do to be successful? Do you have the grit, the determination, and perseverance to see this through?

- **Are there legal or regulatory considerations in your industry?** Many industries, like healthcare or education, come with strict regulations. In my business, we are heavily regulated by the Department of Health's Office of Emergency Medical Services, as well as our national accreditor, CAAHEP. Understanding these requirements early on will help you avoid potential roadblocks.

- **Do you have the necessary skills to run the business?** Entrepreneurship often requires a diverse skill set. You might already have strong problem-solving and leadership skills, but there could be gaps you need to fill. I've often joked that I had to get, as we say here in Massachusetts, "wicked *smaaat*" real quick when I transitioned from teaching to running the business side of our school. This book will help you do the same. I'll share the lessons I learned along the way to help you navigate your journey with a quicker learning curve than I faced.

By evaluating these factors, you'll determine not only whether your business idea is exciting, but also whether it's achievable. Remember, entrepreneurship is a journey that requires careful planning, adaptability, and resilience. The best ideas are those that solve real-world problems and are supported by a well-thought-out strategy.

Moving Forward

Now that you've begun the process of identifying and evaluating business ideas, you're ready to take the next step. In the following chapters, we'll dive deeper into how to create a business plan, define your product or service, and develop strategies for marketing, sales, and growth.

As a first responder, you already have the mindset and the skills needed to face challenges head-on. Entrepreneurship is no different. It requires persistence, adaptability, and a willingness to learn and evolve. But with your background, you're more than capable of navigating this path.

Let's continue this journey together and build something meaningful, both for you and for those you aim to serve.

Now that you've begun shaping your business idea and validating its potential, it's time to move from concept to structure. Your next step is to legally establish your business. It will become the foundation that will support everything you build from here on out. Just like choosing the right tool for the job in the field, selecting the right business structure is important. It determines how you're taxed, how much personal liability you carry, and how you'll be able to grow and scale.

In the next chapter, we'll dive into two of the most common options for new business owners to start their new company: the LLC and the S Corporation. Whether you plan to stay small and agile or scale to something much larger, understanding these structures will help you make decisions that protect your future and position your business for long-term success. Let's explore what's best for you and your vision.

CHAPTER 3

Incorporating Your Business—Choosing Between an LLC and an S Corporation

Incorporating your business is a foundational step that establishes its legal and financial structure, offering both protection and potential advantages. For first responders transitioning into entrepreneurship, understanding how to structure your business can feel overwhelming. Two of the most popular options are the **limited liability company (LLC)** and the **S corporation (S corp)**, each with unique benefits depending on your goals, business complexity, and growth trajectory.

This chapter breaks down the key features, benefits, and considerations for both structures, empowering you to make an informed decision that aligns with your vision.

What is an LLC?

A limited liability company (LLC) blends the simplicity of a partnership with the liability protections of a corporation. It's designed to offer flexibility in management, taxation, and profit-sharing, making it ideal for small businesses and startups.

Key Features of an LLC

- **Personal Liability Protection**: Members' personal assets (homes, savings, etc.) are typically shielded from business debts and lawsuits.

- **Flexible Taxation**: By default, LLCs are pass-through entities, meaning profits and losses flow through to members' personal tax returns. LLCs can also elect to be taxed as an S corp or C corp for additional tax strategies. This is beyond the scope of this book and would require you to consult your tax professional.

- **Simplified Management**: LLCs have fewer formalities than corporations. For example, there's no requirement for annual shareholder meetings or a board of directors.

- **Flexible Profit Distribution**: Members can split profits in ways that don't necessarily align with ownership percentages, allowing for customizable arrangements.

Advantages of an LLC

1. **Ease of Formation**: Establishing an LLC is generally straightforward, involving less paperwork and fewer ongoing compliance requirements than a corporation.

2. **Flexibility**: LLCs adapt to a variety of needs, whether you're a sole proprietor or have multiple members.

3. **Startup-Friendly**: Ideal for first responders balancing full-time work with entrepreneurial ventures, an LLC offers simplicity without sacrificing liability protection.

What is an S Corporation?

An S corporation (S corp) is a specific type of business structure that offers the legal protections of a corporation while avoiding the burden of double taxation. In a traditional C corporation, the business first pays corporate income tax on its profits. Then, when those profits are distributed to shareholders in the form of dividends, the shareholders must also pay personal income tax on that same money. This results in the profits being taxed twice, once at the corporate level and again at the individual level.

An S corporation, however, bypasses this issue. It allows income, deductions, losses, and tax credits to flow directly through the business to the owners' personal tax returns. The business itself does not pay federal income tax, meaning the profits are only taxed once at the shareholder level. This pass-through taxation structure can significantly reduce the overall tax burden, making the S corporation especially appealing for businesses that are generating consistent profits and want to maximize tax efficiency while still enjoying the legal protections of a corporate structure.

Key Features of an S Corp

- **Pass-Through Taxation**: Like an LLC, an S corp avoids corporate taxes, allowing profits to flow directly to shareholders.

- **Salary and Dividends Structure**: Shareholder-employees must take a "reasonable salary," subject to payroll taxes, while additional profits can be distributed as dividends, which are not subject to self-employment taxes.

- **Liability Protection**: Shareholders' personal assets are generally protected from business debts or lawsuits.

- **Formal Requirements**: S corps must maintain a board of directors, hold annual meetings, and follow strict record-keeping protocols.

- **Ownership Restrictions**: S corps are limited to 100 shareholders, all of whom must be US citizens or residents, and can only issue one class of stock.

Advantages of an S Corp

1. **Tax Savings**: The ability to split income between salary and dividends can reduce self-employment taxes, leading to significant tax savings for profitable businesses.

2. **Credibility**: Incorporating as an S corp can enhance your business's reputation, signaling a formal, well-structured organization to clients and partners.

3. **Growth-Friendly**: For businesses anticipating rapid growth, the S corp structure supports scaling while maintaining tax efficiencies.

LLC vs. S Corp: Key Differences

Here's a side-by-side comparison to help you understand the differences between LLCs and S corps:

Feature	LLC	S Corp
Ownership Flexibility	Unlimited members, including corporations and foreign entities	Limited to 100 shareholders, and only US citizens/residents
Taxation	Pass-through by default; can elect S corp or C corp taxation	Pass-through taxation; no corporate taxes
Profit Distribution	Flexible	Based on ownership shares
Management	Flexible; fewer formalities	Requires board of directors and formal meetings
Self-Employment Tax	All income subject to self-employment tax	Salary subject to payroll tax; dividends exempt
Complexity	Simple to set up and manage	More complex setup and compliance requirements

Choosing the Right Structure for Your Business

When to Choose an LLC

- You're looking for simplicity and ease of management.
- You have multiple owners and want flexibility in profit distribution.
- Your business is in its early stages, and you need a structure that can adapt as you grow.
- You're starting a solo business alongside your full-time first responder role.

When to Choose an S Corp

- Your business generates substantial profit, and you want to minimize self-employment taxes.
- You're prepared to manage the additional compliance and formalities required by S corps.
- You're taking a salary as an owner-employee and have the resources to manage payroll taxes.
- Your long-term goals include building a formalized, credible structure for growth.

A Personal Example: Why I Chose an S Corporation

When I launched my business, I chose to incorporate as an S corporation because I saw the potential for significant growth and wanted a structure that could support that trajectory while offering key financial advantages. The decision came after careful consideration of my long-term goals, projected revenue, and the company's operational needs. I wasn't just thinking about how to launch; I was thinking about how to grow, scale, and protect what I was building.

One of the major reasons I selected the S corp structure was the tax strategy it allowed. As an S corp owner, I'm required to pay myself a reasonable salary and run payroll, which is subject to standard payroll taxes. However, profits beyond that salary can be distributed as dividends, which are not subject to self-employment tax. That distinction can result in substantial tax savings once your business becomes profitable. In other words, I could reduce my overall tax burden in a way that allowed me to reinvest more money back into the business.

Yes, S corps come with added responsibilities, payroll, corporate record keeping, and tighter compliance. But those were small trade-offs for the advantages it provided. Choosing the right structure isn't just about where you are now, it's about anticipating where you're going. For my business, the S corp structure became a powerful foundation that supported our evolution into a multimillion-dollar organization. If you're serious about growth and ready to think strategically about taxes and scalability, it's an option worth considering.

Practical Steps to Incorporate

1. **Evaluate Your Needs**: Consider your business's complexity, growth potential, and the type of liability protection you need.

2. **Choose a Platform**: For straightforward setups, services like LegalZoom can simplify the process. For more complex businesses, consult an attorney to ensure all bases are covered.

3. **File the Paperwork**: Submit the necessary forms to your state, including articles of incorporation for an LLC or S corp election for tax purposes (Form 2553).

4. **Obtain an EIN**: Apply for an Employer Identification Number (EIN) through the IRS to handle payroll and tax filings.

5. **Set Up Systems**: Establish payroll (for S corps), accounting software, and any other systems needed to manage your operations efficiently.

The Flexibility of Transitioning from LLC to S Corp

One of the benefits of starting as an LLC is that you can transition to an S corp as your business grows. This allows you to keep the operational simplicity of an LLC early on while taking advantage of S corp tax benefits when your income increases.

Steps to Elect S Corp Status:

1. File Form 2553 with the IRS to elect S corp tax treatment.
2. Implement payroll for yourself as an owner-employee.
3. Ensure compliance with ownership and operational requirements.

Chapter Thoughts

Incorporating your business isn't just about checking a box, it's about laying a solid foundation for long-term success. Whether you opt for an LLC because of its operational simplicity or choose an S corporation to take advantage of potential tax benefits, your decision should be based on your specific goals, business model, and vision for the future.

But incorporation is only the beginning. As your business begins to generate revenue and turn a profit, it's important to start thinking strategically about taxes. Many new business owners wait until tax season to seek help, but by then, it's often too late to take advantage of meaningful strategies that could reduce their tax burden. This is where proactive tax planning becomes essential.

It may be necessary to hire a tax professional who specializes not just in filing returns, but in developing year-round tax strategies tailored to your business. This isn't your typical tax preparer; it's someone who understands how to evaluate your financials, navigate the complexities of tax law, and design a custom plan to minimize your exposure. The key is to engage this kind of help early enough in the year to actually implement the strategies they recommend.

By building tax planning into your business strategy, you're not only protecting your profits, you're setting yourself up for sustained financial growth and stability. Incorporation gives your business legitimacy and structure, but smart tax planning ensures you keep more of what you earn. With your business now legally established and your financial framework beginning to take shape, you've taken a serious step toward turning your vision into a reality. But structure alone won't get you where you want to go. Just like every emergency response begins with a clear tactical and strategic plan, your business also needs a roadmap.

In the next chapter, we'll walk through the process of building your business plan—a blueprint that gives shape to your vision, defines your goals, and helps guide your day-to-day decisions. Whether your idea is still forming or you're already underway, this plan will help you stay focused, resilient, and ready to grow.

CHAPTER 4

Building Your Foundation—Crafting a Solid Business Plan

Now that you've started identifying potential business ideas and evaluating their feasibility, it's time to put those ideas into action with a solid plan. Just as every emergency call demands a well-thought-out strategy and coordinated response, your business needs a structured plan to succeed. A business plan isn't just a formality; it's the roadmap that guides your decisions, secures funding, and keeps you on track toward your goals. In this chapter, we'll break down how to build a business plan that sets you up for long-term success.

| Why a Business Plan Matters

As a first responder, preparation is second nature. You know that going into a situation without a plan can lead to chaos. The same principle applies to launching and running a business. A business plan is your blueprint: it outlines your strategy, identifies potential challenges, and keeps you focused on your objectives.

Beyond providing structure, a well-crafted business plan is also an essential tool for securing financing or investment. Whether you're pitching to investors, applying for a loan, or demonstrating your idea's viability to potential partners, a clear, detailed business plan shows that you've thought everything through and are ready for the challenge.

▌Key Components of a Business Plan

A comprehensive business plan typically includes these key sections:

1. **Executive Summary**: This is the high-level overview of your business. It should outline your business concept, target market, and the problem your product or service solves. Think of it as your "elevator pitch": concise, compelling, and to the point. Although it's the first section in your plan, write it last so you can draw from all the details you've developed. On a side note, an elevator pitch is a short, compelling summary of your business or idea, delivered in the time it takes to ride an elevator, usually thirty seconds to one minute. It's designed to grab attention, spark interest, and leave the person you're talking to wanting to know more. Think of it like this: Just as you quickly assess a patient's condition during a rapid trauma assessment or deliver a concise report over the radio to dispatch, your elevator pitch is a fast, clear, and effective way of communicating your business idea to potential investors, clients, or partners.

2. **Business Description**: This is the section where you describe your product or service, explain the market needs it addresses, and highlight what sets your business apart. Don't forget to include your unique qualifications as a first responder and how your experiences shape your approach. *The First Responder Advantage* highlights your unique background, making you stand out among other businesses.

3. **Market Analysis**: This section is where your research comes in. Identify your target customers, understand their needs, and analyze your competition. Knowing your market is critical. Who are your customers? What do they want, and how can your business meet their needs better than the competition? This analysis will provide a solid foundation for your marketing strategy.

4. **Organization and Management**: Lay out the structure of your business. Who will be involved, and what roles will they play? If you're planning to run the business solo while maintaining your responsibilities as a first responder, explain how you'll manage your time and resources. If you envision building a team, describe your plan for recruiting and managing employees.

5. **Products or Services**: Go into detail about what you're offering. Highlight the features and benefits of your product or service, explaining how it solves a specific problem or fulfills a need. Showcase any unique aspects that give you a competitive advantage. If you have future plans to expand your offerings, mention those as well.

6. **Marketing and Sales Strategy**: Now that you know what you're offering, you need a plan to get it in front of your customers. How will you attract and retain them? Outline your marketing strategy, whether it's social media campaigns, paid ads, or good-old-fashioned word of mouth. Include your sales approach, pricing structure, and promotional plans.

7. **Financial Plan**: This section covers your financial projections and demonstrates the business's potential for profitability. Include revenue forecasts, expense estimates, and profit projections. If you're seeking funding, specify the amount needed and how it

will be used. Be realistic but optimistic; potential investors want to see that your business has growth potential.

8. **Appendixes**: This section is for additional documents that support your plan. It could include market research data, product images, legal documents, or resumes of key team members. Include here anything that strengthens your case.

My First Business Plan

I called my friend, Leslie Hernandez, who worked at the University of Texas Health Science Center (UTHSC). Leslie is a great mentor and helped me in creating the original vision for my first online paramedic class. I explained to her how the school I was teaching at was having some challenges, and that I was going to open my own school. We talked extensively about what I wanted to accomplish in my new business. She told me that UTHSC might be interested in what I was doing, and that she'd speak with her administration.

A few days later, I received a call from Dean Villers. He told me he had spoken with Leslie and he was interested in hearing more about my future plans for our new school. He invited me to "bring my business plan" to Texas in two weeks to meet with him and his team to discuss the new business. As I hung up the phone, I thought to myself, *I have no idea how to write a business plan*, but I had two weeks to figure it out!

I began searching on the internet for how to write a business plan. I found a software program that I could purchase from Staples, which would walk me through the steps and help me fill in the areas needed. For the next two weeks, I dug into planning and creating future goals. I was working twelve to sixteen hours a day on planning for our new business and writing the business plan. I had already committed to opening the school prior to this possible relationship. I had found a space in a commercial office building that I believed could become the school I envisioned, signed a lease, and worked with an architect to design a buildout for the space.

The toughest part of building a business plan was making long-term projections about the business. This is simply guessing! That being said, it is also planning for the future. I had goals, and I needed to be able to articulate those goals to the team at UTHSC. I had to make financial projections as well. I had to think about why UTHSC would want to partner with us. This would be huge for our new school, as having a major university partner put their name on us would give us some instant credibility. If I could secure a relationship with UTHSC, this could be the big break I was looking for.

Revenue Projections

Let's be real for a moment. You might feel like you're dreaming big or perhaps you're being overly optimistic. But maybe you're not. When I started, I had six years of experience teaching paramedic programs, which gave me a solid understanding of the education side of the business. I also had a clear window into the revenue those programs were generating. That firsthand experience and historical data became the foundation for my projections.

From there, it was all about simple math. I asked myself: *If I enrolled a certain number of students at a specific price point, how much revenue would the business generate?* This clarity around what was possible, based on history, logic, and data, helped me build realistic projections and set attainable goals for my business. With a strong foundation in the numbers, I had the confidence to move forward and make it happen.

Setting Goals and Milestones

Once your business plan is in place, the next critical step is translating your long-term vision into manageable, actionable steps. Clear, measurable goals provide a roadmap for progress and ensure you stay focused. For first responders, this approach aligns with the way you operate on deadlines and objectives during emergency calls: each step serves a purpose and brings you closer to the outcome.

A powerful way to structure your goals is by using the SMART framework. By ensuring each goal is Specific, Measurable, Achievable, Relevant, and Time-Bound, you can create a clear path forward and set yourself up for success.

What Are SMART Goals?

- **Specific**: Define exactly what you want to achieve.
- **Measurable**: Determine how success will be quantified.
- **Achievable**: Ensure the goal is realistic, given your resources.
- **Relevant**: Align the goal with your overall business vision and objectives.
- **Time-Bound**: Set a clear deadline to maintain urgency and accountability.

Breaking Down Your Goals

| Short-Term Goals: Laying the Foundation

- o Short-term goals are focused on immediate priorities that help you establish your business and gain momentum.

- **Example**: "Develop a prototype or basic version of my service within three months."

- **SMART Breakdown**:

  - o *Specific*: Create a working prototype of the service.

  - o *Measurable*: Complete the prototype by the end of the quarter.

  - o *Achievable*: Allocate ten hours per week to design and development.

  - o *Relevant*: A prototype is critical to presenting the service to potential clients.

  - o *Time-Bound*: Deadline: Three months.

Whenever I embarked on a new project or set out to complete a challenging task, I relied on a structured framework to lay out my goals and establish a clear timeline. This wasn't just about organization, it was about creating a system of personal accountability. Setting deadlines and breaking down objectives helped me stay focused and ensured progress wasn't left to chance.

But I didn't stop there. I took it a step further by sharing my goals with others, whether it was my team, friends, or family. This external layer of accountability fueled my determination. As someone who takes pride in being true to my word, telling others about my objectives created a powerful sense of responsibility. Once I vocalized my intentions, there was no turning back. I felt compelled to push through distractions, doubts, or obstacles because I had made a promise, not just to myself, but to those who were now watching.

This sense of commitment became the extra push I often needed to overcome challenges and complete my projects. It transformed my goals from private ambitions into public commitments, adding just enough pressure to stay driven while reinforcing my integrity as a leader.

Medium-Term Goals: Building and Testing

Medium-term goals focus on refining your offering and gathering feedback to improve its quality and value.

- **Example**: "Test the new design of our EMT program with fifty students and gather feedback within six months."

- **SMART Breakdown**:

  o *Specific*: Launch new EMT program.

  o *Measurable*: Track the number of participants and collect feedback forms.

  o *Achievable*: Develop a plan for two cohorts of students to be in the test group.

  o *Relevant*: Feedback will improve the product and validate market demand.

  o *Time-Bound*: Deadline: Six months.

Long-Term Goals: Expanding and Scaling

Long-term goals are designed to grow your business and solidify its place in the market.

- **Example**: "Launch my service to a wider market and scale my business within eighteen months."

- **SMART Breakdown**:

  o *Specific*: Expand to two additional regions or market segments.

  o *Measurable*: Achieve a twenty-five percent increase in customer base and a thirty percent increase in revenue.

  o *Achievable*: Use feedback from the medium-term goal to fine-tune the service and implement a targeted marketing campaign.

  o *Relevant*: Growth aligns with the overall vision of becoming a market leader.

  o *Time-Bound*: Deadline: Eighteen months.

Incorporating Milestones: Celebrating Progress

Each goal should include milestones. These are like waypoints on a map, which act as checkpoints to track progress and maintain momentum. Milestones provide opportunities to celebrate achievements, identify challenges, and adjust your plan if necessary.

- **Short-Term Milestone**: Complete the initial design phase of your prototype within one month.

- **Medium-Term Milestone**: Gather feedback from the first ten customers within two months of launching the test.

- **Long-Term Milestone**: Secure partnerships in new regions within twelve months to support scaling efforts.

Milestones ensure that you're not just focused on the destination but also recognizing the progress you're making along the way. It can also help you understand if you are not on the right track. Creating milestones can help you identify trends and adjust quickly so as not to waste valuable time

Setting SMART goals and milestones provides structure, clarity, and purpose to your entrepreneurial journey. By breaking your long-term vision into achievable steps, you can stay focused, track your progress, and celebrate each milestone along the way. Remember, just like responding to emergencies, success in business comes from preparation, execution, and learning from every experience.

Start today: define your first SMART goal and take the first step toward turning your vision into reality.

Budgeting and Financial Planning

Managing your finances is just as important as creating a great product. You know the importance of allocating resources effectively in your work as a first responder, and that skill translates directly to business. Whether you're using personal savings or seeking external funding, it is essential to create a budget that covers your startup costs and supports sustainable growth.

Identify potential expenses, including:

- Equipment and supplies
- Marketing and advertising
- Legal and accounting fees
- Office space or home office setup
- Technology and software

Once you've outlined your expenses, create realistic revenue projections for your first year. Be conservative in your estimates, especially in the early stages, when revenue can be unpredictable. The goal is to craft a financial plan that fosters growth while maintaining control over spending.

Making Projections: People, Space, and Equipment

After completing your projected revenue potential, the next step is to assess the costs associated with running your business. Understanding and forecasting expenses for people, space, and equipment is essential to building a sustainable operation. Let's break this down into actionable steps so you can make informed decisions and avoid costly surprises.

1. Projecting Costs for People

Your team will be one of the most significant investments in your business. Whether you're hiring employees, contractors, or freelancers, you need a clear understanding of the costs involved.

Key Considerations:

- **Salaries and Wages**: Research industry standards for the roles you need to fill. If you're hiring part-time help or contractors, determine their hourly rates and estimated hours per week. For example, if you're running a training business, you might need instructors, administrative support, or a marketing manager.

- **Benefits and Taxes**: Don't overlook the additional costs of employment, such as health insurance, retirement contributions, payroll taxes, and workers' compensation. These can add up to thirty percent beyond the base salary. A friend of mine who owns an accounting firm had a great spreadsheet that auto-calculated the federal and state taxes and social security, as well as health benefits if you offer them. I just plugged in the hourly wage or salary, and it calculated the true cost of hiring an employee.

Fortunately, there are commercially available spreadsheet templates and online calculators that can help estimate the true cost of hiring. Many of these tools allow you to input hourly wages or salaries and will automatically calculate federal and state taxes, Social Security, Medicare, and optional benefits, giving you a more accurate picture of what each hire will truly cost your business.

- **Training and Onboarding**: Factor in the time and resources required to onboard and train new hires. This includes software licenses, equipment, and the time spent getting them up to speed.

- **Scaling as You Grow**: As your business expands, your personnel needs will likely grow as well. Create a tiered hiring plan that aligns with your revenue milestones. For example, if you hit a target of fifty clients, you might need an additional administrative assistant or another salesperson.

Start Lean, Scale Smart

Starting lean and scaling your team gradually is a proven strategy for early-stage businesses. By outsourcing essential tasks like bookkeeping, graphic design, or marketing, you can save money while accessing professional expertise without the overhead costs of full-time employees. It's a practical approach to building momentum without overextending resources.

A Humble Beginning

April 1, 2010, marked the launch of my company, National Medical Education & Training Center (NMETC). The day felt exhilarating and terrifying in equal parts. It also felt like the biggest April Fools' joke I had ever played on myself. Late in the afternoon on March 31, I received the long-awaited word from our state EMS office: our accreditation had been approved. We were officially allowed to open for business. I immediately called our web designer (a former student) and told him, "Make the website live!"

The next morning, as the website launched, I found myself sitting alone in the school. There were no students or employees—just me in an empty building, staring at my computer screen and wondering, *What did I just do?*

I had envisioned this moment for so long, but when it arrived, the reality hit me like a tidal wave. The weight of taking on something so monumental was both daunting and exhilarating. I had stepped far outside my comfort zone to follow a dream, one that carried endless possibilities but also significant risks. I had leased a 4,000-square-foot space, and as I sat there, the gravity of the situation became crystal clear. The financial stakes were enormous, and I couldn't ignore the fact that I had only two months' worth of lease payments in the bank. If I didn't enroll students quickly, the entire venture could collapse before it even began.

The lease payment alone was more than I earned in a month at my fire department job. The enormity of that realization hit me hard, and I knew there was no room for hesitation. That first day, I sprang into action, emailing contacts, reaching out to friends, and making phone calls to anyone who might be interested or know someone who was. By the end of the day, I had one student enrolled and several others promising to fill out applications. That one student gave me another month of breathing room—a small victory, but a critical one.

I wasn't truly alone in this journey, though. I had an incredible support system. My wife believed in me unconditionally, standing by my side even when the risks seemed overwhelming. My family supported me every step of the way, and a network of friends and educators I'd worked with over the years were ready to jump in as soon as we had students to teach. Their encouragement became my foundation, but the road ahead was mine to pave.

One friend who would later play a pivotal role in our success was Tanya Beaulieu. At the time, Tanya was eager to regain her EMT license, which had lapsed, and she reached out to me about joining our first EMT class. I had to be honest with her: I wasn't even sure the class would run, because we didn't have enough students enrolled. Undeterred, Tanya became a one-woman recruitment machine. She spread the word, rallied friends, and brought in enough people to make our first EMT class possible. Her determination and belief in the program were infectious, and her efforts single-handedly made that class possible.

Today, Tanya serves as our Director of Admissions, playing a vital role in our team's success. Her journey from being one of our first students to becoming a cornerstone of our organization is a testament to the power of resilience, relationships, and unwavering belief in a shared mission.

Looking back, that first day was a whirlwind of fear, action, and a glimmer of hope. It was a day that set the tone for the grit and determination that would carry us through the challenges ahead. The support I had, from my wife, family, and friends like Tanya, reminded me that while the road ahead might be tough, I wasn't walking it alone. Together, we were building something meaningful, and with every small win, the dream came closer to reality.

Publicizing the First Offering

I began to spread the word about our first online paramedic program. This was a groundbreaking concept at the time, taking a traditionally hands-on, in-person training program and moving it online. Skepticism was everywhere. I heard things like, "How do you teach a paramedic program online?" and "That's never going to work." But I knew I was onto something. I'd spent years in the education side of EMS and understood not only the gaps in access to training but also the potential demand for a more flexible learning option. I also had three years of successful online programs under my belt. I had already proven the concept.

With no students yet enrolled, I had to focus on building trust, credibility, and a compelling case for our program. The early days were about knocking on metaphorical doors, sharing the vision, and answering countless questions from potential students, their families, and even skeptics in the EMS field.

Starting Lean

At this stage, I didn't have the luxury of hiring a full-time staff. The budget was tight, and every dollar had to be accounted for. Instead of immediately bringing on full-time employees, I relied on outsourcing and the goodwill of colleagues willing to work on a part-time or contract basis.

- **Bookkeeping**: Rather than hiring an in-house accountant, I tried doing it myself. However, this proved to be some distance outside my wheelhouse. I was a teacher, not a bookkeeper. I used spreadsheets to keep track of all the expenses and revenue. I realized very quickly I needed a better system, as we began to have more and more transactions on both the expenses and the revenue side. Eventually, I used an external bookkeeping service to manage our finances. It was cost-effective and ensured accuracy while freeing me to focus on building the program.

- **Web Design**: The website was a crucial part of our program's success, so I outsourced the design and maintenance to a trusted professional and former student, Eric Lotte. Eric designed an amazing website for me and saved me thousands in design costs! Once it was up and running, it allowed us to present a polished, professional image right from the start without the ongoing cost of an internal developer. I also had access to change the website, so I could self-manage it as necessary.

- **Marketing**: Spreading the word about the program required expertise I didn't have. I partnered with a freelance marketer to create initial campaigns. Prior to leveraging social media posts, I used email outreach and snail-mailed advertising poster cards, which helped us generate leads. If I were starting over today, the power of social media marketing is amazing, and targeting EMTs who might want to be paramedics would be so much easier!

The Moment of Momentum

The tipping point came when we enrolled our first cohort of students. That initial group validated the entire concept in our new school. It proved that the demand was real and sustainable, and that people were ready to embrace a new way of learning. With students enrolled, I could finally start expanding the team. The educators I had worked with in the past joined the mission, and together, we built a program that would go on to impact countless lives.

Starting lean wasn't just a necessity, it became one of the most valuable lessons in entrepreneurship. It forced me to prioritize, focus on what truly mattered, and avoid wasting resources on non-essentials. Looking back, those early days of sitting alone in an empty school weren't just the beginning of a business, they were the foundation of a journey that would grow into something far greater than I could have imagined.

TAKEAWAY FOR FIRST RESPONDERS: Starting a business may feel overwhelming, especially when you're sitting in that metaphorical empty room, wondering what comes next. But if you start lean, rely on your network, and stay focused on your vision, you'll find that each step forward builds momentum. Whether it's outsourcing key tasks, calling on your support system, or simply taking that first leap, remember: every successful business starts with a moment of faith, and continues with a lot of grit.

2. Projecting Costs for Space

The cost of physical space is often one of the largest expenses for a growing business, especially if your operations require a brick-and-mortar presence.

Key Considerations:

- **Rent or Lease**: Research market rates for commercial spaces in your area. Consider whether you'll need a retail storefront, office space, or a warehouse. For example, if you're starting a handyman service, a small office with storage for tools might suffice. If you're running a training school, you may need classrooms, labs, or a larger facility.

- **Utilities and Maintenance**: Don't forget to account for electricity, heating, cooling, internet, cleaning, and other operational costs associated with your space.

- **Flexibility for Growth**: Consider whether the space will accommodate future growth. Signing a short-term lease initially can provide flexibility while you assess your long-term needs.

- **Buildout Costs:** When leasing a commercial space, especially one that's not move-in ready for your specific type of business, buildout costs—also known as tenant improvements—can be a significant expense. These are the costs associated with modifying or customizing the space to meet the operational needs of your business.

For example, if you're opening a training center, you might need to build out classrooms, install A/V equipment, create administrative offices, set up workstations, or add specialized storage areas. Each of these improvements requires materials, labor, permitting, and potentially inspections, all of which come with a price tag.

Why It Matters

These costs can quickly add up and, if not accounted for in your startup projections, may eat into your capital or delay your launch timeline.

That's why it's critical to include estimated buildout expenses in your financial planning from the beginning.

Negotiating Buildout Allowances

If you're signing a longer-term lease, typically three years or more, you may be in a position to negotiate with the landlord for a **tenant improvement (TI) allowance**. This is a financial contribution from the landlord toward the cost of your buildout. Sometimes this is offered as a dollar-per-square-foot allowance; other times it might come as rent abatement (a few months of free or reduced rent) to offset the costs you'll incur.

When negotiating, make sure:

- You get the agreement in writing
- You understand what expenses are covered
- You're clear on who oversees the construction; some landlords will want to manage the improvements themselves, while others will allow you to hire your own contractors.

In all three of the spaces we have leased, each of the buildouts was handled by the landlord. Our current space requires a significant buildout of 18,000 sq/ft. There are significant advantages to this, including having your capital outlay for the buildout to be as minimal as possible. We signed a ten-year lease, so it gave us a significant negotiating position. It was a win-win for both of us. The landlord got a long-term commitment in a monthly lease, and we negotiated an expensive buildout of our new school, where our out-of-pocket expenses were less than ten percent of the total cost of the construction. It did increase our monthly cost over time, but it was well worth it when I conducted the analysis of the entire lease.

If you are using your own capital (this will usually keep your per sq/ft cost lower), consider phasing your buildout to manage costs. Start with the essentials that allow you to open your doors and generate revenue, then upgrade or expand as cash flow allows.

By properly estimating and planning for buildout costs and negotiating support where you can, you'll protect your budget and set the stage for a functional, professional space that supports your business goals from day one.

> **PRO TIP:** Negotiate with landlords. Many property owners are willing to offer incentives like reduced rent for the first few months or buildout credits, especially for long-term leases.

3. Projecting Costs for Equipment

Equipment costs can vary significantly depending on your industry. Whether you're investing in tools for a handyman business, technology for a training school, or vehicles for a delivery service, you'll need to plan carefully.

Key Considerations:

- **Initial Equipment Purchases**: List all the essential equipment you'll need to get started. For example, a training school might require computers, projectors or TVs, mannequins, and simulation tools, while a handyman business might need power tools, ladders, and work vehicles.

- **Replacement and Upgrades**: Equipment doesn't last forever. Plan for regular maintenance and eventual replacement of critical items. If you're using technology, remember that software and hardware will need updates over time.

- **Leasing vs. Buying**: For high-cost items like vehicles or large machinery, consider whether leasing is a better option than purchasing outright. Leasing can free up capital and allow for easier upgrades, though it may cost more over the long term.

- **Technology and Software**: In addition to physical equipment, account for the cost of software, subscriptions, and licenses. For instance, you may need accounting software, customer relationship management (CRM) tools, or industry-specific programs. Shop around for these products, as they vary greatly in cost and complexity of use. Talk with other business owners to see what they are using for systems.

- **Inventory Needs**: If your business involves selling physical products, include the cost of inventory in your equipment projections. This includes initial stock as well as ongoing replenishment.

Bringing It All Together

Once you've projected the costs for people, space, and equipment, you'll have a clearer picture of your business's financial needs. Combine these projections with your revenue estimates to create a detailed budget that includes:

- **Fixed Costs:** Expenses that don't vary with business activity, such as rent, salaries, and insurance.

- **Variable Costs:** Expenses that fluctuate based on business activity, such as materials, utilities, and shipping.

- **One-Time Costs:** Initial setup expenses, such as equipment purchases, legal fees, or build-outs.

This budget will serve as your financial roadmap, helping you make informed decisions, prioritize investments, and avoid surprises.

PRO TIP: Shop smart for equipment. Consider shopping for used or refurbished equipment to save money without compromising quality.

For example, secondhand tools, office furniture, or even technology can significantly reduce upfront costs while still meeting your needs.

When starting my business, I knew we needed a high-speed printer/copier/scanner/fax machine—a workhorse that could handle our day-to-day operations. But these machines were expensive, and with money tight, I needed an alternative. That's when I began searching for refurbished options and found **Copitex**, a small business specializing in selling and leasing refurbished machines.

The owner, **Mike Kates**, was based in the same town where I worked as a firefighter. From our first conversation, I could tell Mike was someone who understood the challenges of starting a business. He didn't just try to sell me the most expensive equipment; he took the time to understand what I truly needed and what would work within my budget.

Mike set me up with a lease-to-own deal. This approach kept my upfront costs low, which was critical during the startup phase, and allowed me to make manageable monthly payments. Not only did this save much-needed startup capital, but it also gave me access to a high-quality machine that supported our growing operations.

This experience reinforced the importance of building relationships with other small business owners. By working with someone like Mike, who understood the unique pressures of launching a business, I gained not just equipment, but also a trusted partner.

KEY TAKEAWAY: When shopping for equipment, don't underestimate the value of local businesses and refurbished options. By seeking out creative solutions like leasing or purchasing secondhand, you can stretch your budget and focus your resources where they're needed most, growing your business.

Preparing for the Unexpected

Just as no emergency call unfolds exactly as expected, the entrepreneurial journey is filled with surprises. Your business plan should include contingency plans for dealing with unexpected challenges. What if your product doesn't sell as quickly as anticipated? What if unexpected expenses arise? Planning for these scenarios helps mitigate risks and ensures you stay focused on your long-term goals.

Startup Business Plan Example

Here is an example of what a startup business plan could look like. Remember, business plans can range from highly detailed to straightforward and concise. The key is to avoid getting trapped in endless planning at the expense of taking action. Too often, I've seen aspiring entrepreneurs spend so much time perfecting their plans that they never move forward and launch their business. Use this example as a guide, but don't let the planning phase hold you back. Real progress comes when you execute your idea and bring your vision to life.

| Business Plan for Solid Solutions Handyman Services

Executive Summary: Solid Solutions Handyman Services specializes in custom shed construction, porch building, and general repair work. Rooted in the values of reliability, integrity, and service, our company leverages the owner's experience as a first responder to build trust and deliver exceptional quality. With years of hands-on experience in construction and repair, Solid Solutions aims to serve homeowners and small businesses seeking high-quality structures and dependable repair work at competitive prices.

Business Description: Solid Solutions Handyman Services caters to residential and light commercial clients. Our core offerings include:

- Custom shed building
- Porch construction
- General home and light commercial repair services

The owner's background as a first responder has instilled qualities that form the backbone of the business: quick thinking, reliability, and the ability to stay calm under pressure. These traits translate directly to efficient, trustworthy service, where clients feel confident that their projects are in capable hands.

Market Analysis: The market for handyman and small-scale construction services is strong, driven by an increasing trend in home improvement projects and property value investments. Our target customers include homeowners looking for custom storage solutions, enhanced outdoor spaces, or reliable repair services. Competitors include small local contractors and larger construction firms that often overlook smaller jobs.

Organization and Management: Solid Solutions is owned and operated by John Smith, a licensed contractor and former first responder with over fifteen years of experience in residential construction. The discipline, teamwork, and commitment to service honed through years of emergency response have equipped John with a unique approach to customer interaction and project management. Part-time employees will be hired during peak construction seasons to support growing demand.

Products or Services

1. **Custom Sheds**: Fully customizable sheds, from basic storage units to more elaborate structures.

2. **Porch Construction**: High-quality porches that add functional and aesthetic value to outdoor spaces.

3. **Repair Work**: Comprehensive repair services that cover carpentry, minor electrical fixes, and general home maintenance.

Marketing and Sales Strategy

- **Trust-Based Marketing**: Emphasizing the owner's background as a first responder to highlight reliability and commitment.

- **Online Presence**: A website featuring completed projects, customer testimonials, and service descriptions.

- **Community Engagement**: Participation in local events and partnerships with real estate agents and home improvement stores for referrals.

- **Social Media Campaigns**: Regularly posting project updates and home improvement tips to build engagement.

- **Direct Marketing**: Fliers and business cards distributed in key residential areas.

Financial Plan Startup Costs:

- Equipment and tools: $10,000
- Vehicle for transportation: $15,000 (used truck)
- Initial inventory (lumber, fasteners, etc.): $5,000
- Marketing (website, fliers, etc.): $2,000
- Licensing and insurance: $3,000

Total Startup Costs: $35,000

Revenue Projections (Year 1):

- Custom shed projects (15 sheds at $4,000 each): $60,000
- Porch construction (10 porches at $7,500 each): $75,000
- Repair work (monthly average of $2,500): $30,000

Total Projected Revenue: $165,000

Expense Projections (Year 1):

- Labor costs (part-time helpers): $40,000
- Materials: $40,000
- Insurance and licensing renewal: $3,000
- Marketing and advertising: $4,000
- Vehicle maintenance and fuel: $5,000
- Miscellaneous expenses: $3,000

Total Projected Expenses: $95,000

Projected Profit (Year 1): **Net Profit**: $165,000 (revenue) - $95,000 (expenses) = **$70,000**

Appendixes

- Detailed list of tools and equipment.
- Sample shed and porch designs.
- Owner's résumé with first responder and construction experience.

Setting Goals and Milestones: Solid Solutions is built on the values of trust, dedication, and skill that come from years of service as a first responder. Setting actionable goals ensures the business stays aligned with those values:

- **Short-term goal**: Complete five projects in the first three months to build a strong reputation and secure referrals.

- **Medium-term goal**: Expand services to include deck restoration and additional handyman offerings.

- **Long-term goal**: Hire a full-time team and scale operations to serve a wider area, taking on more advanced projects such as small home additions.

Solid Solutions Handyman Services is more than a business, it's a reflection of the trust and integrity that first responders embody. Our commitment to quality workmanship and dependable service aims to build lasting relationships with clients. By applying the discipline and dedication learned from years in the field, Solid Solutions is positioned for sustainable growth and long-term success.

Chapter Thoughts

A solid business plan is the foundation of successful entrepreneurship. As a first responder, you already understand the value of preparation, strategy, and adaptability. By applying these strengths to your business plan, you'll be equipped to turn your idea into reality and navigate the path ahead with confidence.

In the next chapter, we'll shift our focus to building your brand and establishing your presence in the market. We'll explore how to communicate your vision effectively, connect with your audience, and create a memorable brand that sets you apart.

Let's take the next step together as you build a strong foundation for your entrepreneurial future.

CHAPTER 5

Building Your Brand—Creating a Strong Market Presence

Once you have your business plan in place, the next step is to build a solid brand and make your business stand out in the market. Think of your brand as the connection between what you offer and the people who need it. It's how you express who you are, build trust, and shape how customers see you. As a first responder, you already know the importance of a good reputation, and it's the same for your business: it's what makes people trust you in emergencies. Your brand is more than just a cool logo or a catchy phrase; it's the whole story of your business, the values you live by, and the experience you create for your customers. A strong brand not only helps you stand out from the crowd but also gives your team something to be proud of and shows what your business is all about.

The Power of Intentional Branding

I used to think we had a great brand. Our message was on point, our mission was clear, and we lived our principles in every class we taught. But as we expanded, things started to feel a bit disjointed. Our branding wasn't consistent or intentional enough. Then, in 2023, we brought Dan Limmer onto our team as the Director of Innovation. Dan is a legend in EMS education, the author of the EMT textbook we use, and a successful entrepreneur himself. He and his wife, Stephanie, run Limmer Education, a company with apps that help EMS students prep for their certification exams. Dan brought a ton of branding experience to our team, thanks to his own company and his work in publishing.

Soon after joining us, Dan pointed out a blind spot I had: our branding was all over the place. We had two different logos for our school, which was confusing. Our instructors were creating presentations in whatever style they liked, leading to a real mix of visuals. Some were great, others...not so much. Even though we had a clear mission, the inconsistent look of our materials diluted our message. Dan's expertise in branding was a game-changer for us. He highlighted the need for a unified brand identity and how it could boost our reputation and improve the student experience. It was a much-needed realization. We had to step up our game, not just for appearances but to make sure everything we did reflected our mission and values.

Building a Brand That Clicks

A strong brand doesn't just magically appear. It takes planning and a deep understanding of your goals, your audience, and what you stand for. In this chapter, we'll explore the key parts of creating a brand that connects with your audience, shows your values, and sets you up for success.

What Exactly is a Brand?

A brand is more than just a logo or a slogan. It captures the entire experience your customers have with your business. It's your mission, vision, values, and how you present yourself to the world, all rolled into one. It's like a promise to your customers, telling them what they can always expect from you. As a first responder, you inherently bring values like trust, reliability, and service to your business. These qualities instantly build credibility and show that you're the real deal. They're not just ideas; they're what people expect from first responders, and they can be the foundation of your business reputation.

If you visited our school today, you'd see our brand in action. We've designed our space to show our dedication to education and to creating a great experience for everyone who walks through our doors. From classrooms to common areas, everything aims to project professionalism and care. But our brand goes beyond the physical space. It's in the friendly welcome, the genuine connections our team builds with students, and the sense of community we foster. We want every student to feel valued, supported, and sure that they've made the right choice by joining our program.

A strong brand shows who you are, what you believe in, and how much you care about serving your customers. It's not just about appearances; it's about how you make people feel. Every interaction, online or in-person, should reinforce the trust and professionalism that define your brand. When your customers see those values, your brand becomes a powerful way to build relationships, keep customers coming back, and achieve long-term success.

Defining Your Brand Identity

To build a strong brand, you need to start with a clear identity. This means answering some fundamental questions about what your business stands for and how you want to be perceived:

- **Mission**: What's the purpose of your business? What problems are you solving, and why does your business exist? Your mission should reflect the core values that drive you as both a first responder and an entrepreneur.

- **Vision**: Where do you see your business in the future? What kind of impact do you want to make? A clear vision helps guide your brand strategy and ensures that all business decisions align with your long-term goals.

- **Values**: What principles guide your business? As a first responder, values like integrity, professionalism, and dedication are part of who you are. Make those values visible in your brand to attract customers who share similar beliefs.

- **Target Audience**: Who are your ideal customers, and what do they care about? Understanding your audience is critical. Consider what motivates them, the challenges they face, and how your business provides solutions that resonate with them.

Crafting Your Brand's Message

Your brand message is how you communicate your identity to the world. It should be clear, consistent, and reflective of the values you want to convey. Think of it as your business's story. It shows what you stand for, what makes you different, and why customers should choose you.

Here are a few key components of a strong brand message:

- **Tagline**: A short, memorable phrase that captures the essence of your business. It should be simple and meaningful, giving potential customers a sense of what you offer at a glance.

  o At our business, we have "Get Trained, Get Certified, Make a Difference."

    o   We also have "Education without Borders."

- **Value Proposition**: This is your core promise to customers, demonstrating why they should choose your business over others. It highlights the benefits of your product or service and explains how you solve their problems. Make sure this value proposition is featured prominently in your marketing materials, from your website to social media pages.

- **Brand Voice**: How you communicate is just as important as what you communicate. Your brand voice should align with your business's personality and values. As a first responder, your voice may naturally be authoritative, reassuring, and solution-focused—qualities that inspire trust and confidence.

Designing Your Visual Identity

Once you've defined your brand message, it's time to focus on the visual elements that represent your business. This includes your logo, color scheme, typography, and overall design style. A consistent and professional visual identity is key to making a lasting impression and building brand recognition.

Tips for Developing Your Visual Identity:

- **Simplicity**: A clean, simple design is often the most effective. Your logo and other visual elements should be easy to recognize and remember. Avoid clutter or overly complicated designs that might confuse your audience.

- **Consistency**: Consistency is crucial for building trust and recognition. Use the same colors, fonts, and design style across all your marketing materials. This creates a cohesive and professional image for your business.

- **Relevance**: Your visual identity should align with the nature of your business. For example, if your business focuses on safety consulting, consider bold and trustworthy colors like blue or green. If you're in a creative field, brighter, more dynamic visuals might be a better fit. Whatever you choose, ensure it matches your brand's values and message. We redesigned our logo two years ago to align better with who we are now compared to who we were in 2010. I was worried about the logo shift. However, we have incorporated it into our school and have slowly phased it into all areas of our business. We still have a legacy sign with our original logo at our entrance to remind us where we came from.

PRO TIP: Harness the power of global talent for your logo design.

Creating a standout logo is a critical step in establishing your brand identity, and outsourcing to freelance designers can open the door to innovative and diverse ideas.

Platforms like DesignCrowd or ZillionDesigns offer fantastic solutions by connecting you with a global network of talented designers. Here's how it works:

1. **Post Your Project**: Share the details of your logo requirements, including your business name, industry, style preferences, and any specific elements you'd like incorporated.

2. **Receive Multiple Designs**: Freelance designers from around the world will compete to create the perfect logo for your business.

You'll receive a variety of unique concepts tailored to your specifications.

3. **Provide Feedback**: Collaborate with designers by giving feedback to refine the designs. This interactive process ensures the final product aligns with your vision.

4. **Choose Your Favorite**: Once all submissions are in, you pick the design that best represents your brand.

These types of platforms make it easy to tap into a wide range of creative talent, providing you with many options for your logo. Not only does this approach give you fresh perspectives, but it's also cost-effective and flexible. Take your time reviewing designs, and don't hesitate to ask for revisions to ensure your logo is a perfect reflection of your brand. A memorable logo sets the tone for your business and leaves a lasting impression on your audience!

Creating Your Online Presence

In today's digital world, having an online presence is essential for any business. Most of your customers will find you online, whether through social media, online reviews, or your own website. Building a strong online presence allows you to reach a wider audience, showcase your brand, and establish credibility.

1. Website: Your website is your digital storefront, often the first place potential customers go to learn more about you. Ensure your website is professional, easy to navigate, and conveys your brand message clearly. Include details about your products or services, your mission, and contact information. A blog or news section can help keep your audience engaged and updated on your business.

In the early stages of our business, I recognized the importance of having a professional and functional website. I knew many potential students would discover us through an internet search, so it was important to create a site that not only introduced them to who we were and what we offered but also provided real functionality behind the scenes. Our website wasn't just a digital storefront, it was a direct gateway to our programs.

A key feature was a clear sales call-to-action button labeled "Enroll Now," designed to make it easy for students to apply to our program. With just a click, they were taken to an application page where they could provide their information and pay an application fee upon submission. This streamlined process ensured that our website served as both a welcoming first impression and an efficient tool for driving enrollment. It became a vital part of our business strategy, transforming interest into action with ease.

We have had multiple versions of our website over the years. The last redesign we did several years ago was based on Donald Miller's book *StoryBrand*. Miller's StoryBrand framework revolutionizes the way businesses approach advertising by focusing on storytelling that centers the customer as the hero. At its core, the framework helps businesses clarify their message so it resonates deeply with their audience. Miller emphasizes that every successful brand story follows a familiar structure: a hero (the customer) encounters a problem, meets a guide (your business), who provides a plan to overcome the challenge, leading to a positive transformation.

The brilliance of StoryBrand lies in its simplicity. Instead of inundating potential customers with confusing details about products or services, businesses are taught to craft a clear and compelling narrative that answers three key questions: What problem are you solving? How can you help? What success will the customer achieve? By positioning the customer as the hero and the brand as a trusted guide, Miller's approach builds trust, clarifies the value proposition, and ultimately drives engagement and sales. It's a method that feels personal, actionable, and highly effective, particularly in a world overwhelmed by noise in advertising. We have adopted StoryBrand in every aspect of our business.

2. Social Media: Platforms like Facebook, Instagram, LinkedIn, Twitter (X), and TikTok are powerful tools for building your brand and connecting with your audience. The key is to select the platforms that align with your business and to post consistent, high-quality content. Sharing updates, success stories, customer testimonials, and behind-the-scenes glimpses can foster trust and loyalty with your audience.

Our business was initially slow to embrace social media. Most of our students came to us through word of mouth, and our alumni became our strongest advocates, sharing their experiences with others. They talked about how they were treated at our school, the quality of education they received, and how well-prepared they felt for the National Registry Exam and their careers. This organic growth drove our success year after year.

Eventually, we realized that building our social media presence wasn't just about attracting new students; it was about shaping our brand. To achieve this, we hired a social media consultant to help us craft a consistent brand message across all our platforms. This step allowed us to reach a broader audience while staying true to the values and quality that had built our reputation.

3. Online Reviews: Positive reviews are one of the most powerful tools for building credibility. Encourage satisfied customers to leave reviews on Google, Yelp, or industry-specific platforms. Respond to all reviews— positive and negative—with professionalism and care, showing potential customers that you value feedback and strive for excellence. On social media, never get into an argument with anyone. For your business's sake, just stay out of the noise.

Leveraging Your First Responder Experience

As a first responder, you bring a unique set of skills and experiences to your business. Don't be afraid to highlight this in your branding. Your ability to stay calm under pressure, your commitment to serving the community, and your understanding of people's needs set you apart from competitors.

Consider weaving your first responder background into your brand story. For example, if you're launching a safety consulting service, emphasize your hands-on experience in high-stress emergency situations and how it informs your approach. This not only builds credibility but positions you as an expert with real-world knowledge.

Chapter Thoughts

Building a strong brand is an essential part of establishing your business and making a lasting impression in the market. It's how you communicate who you are, what you stand for, and why customers should choose you. As a first responder, you have the values of trust, reliability, and service already ingrained in you, qualities that translate seamlessly into a successful brand identity.

In the next chapter, we'll explore effective marketing and sales strategies, focusing on how to reach your target audience, generate leads, and turn potential customers into loyal clients. You're already on your way to building something remarkable—let's keep going.

CHAPTER 6

Reaching Your Audience—Marketing and Sales Strategies for First Responders

Now that you've built a strong brand and established your business identity, the next step is learning how to reach your audience and generate sales. Marketing and sales are the lifeblood of any business; no matter how exceptional your product or service is, it won't make an impact unless people know it exists and are motivated to buy it. As a first responder, you understand the importance of preparation, strategy, and execution, principles that are just as vital in business as they are on the job. In this chapter, we'll explore how to develop marketing strategies that resonate with your target audience and effective sales techniques that turn leads into customers.

Understanding Your Target Audience

The foundation of any successful marketing strategy is knowing who your audience is and what they care about. Just as you approach every emergency situation with a clear understanding of the people involved and the environment, your marketing efforts need to be tailored to the specific needs, preferences, and behaviors of your target market/audience.

Key Questions to Define Your Audience

Start by asking these questions:

- **Who is your ideal customer?** Be as specific as possible when defining your target audience. Are you targeting individuals, businesses, or organizations? What are their demographics (age, location, profession, etc.)? For instance, if your business focuses on home safety consulting, your ideal customer might be homeowners aged thirty–sixty who prioritize family safety.

- **What problems are they facing?** Your product or service should be a solution to a problem your audience is experiencing. Understanding their pain points allows you to position your business as the answer they've been looking for. For example, if your business provides online EMT training, you're addressing the issue of limited access to traditional classes.

- **Where do they spend their time?** Knowing where your target audience spends time—both online and offline—will help you choose the best marketing channels. Are they active on social media? Do they read industry-specific publications? Are they likely to attend community events or conferences?

Two of the firefighters on my shift, Corbett and Joey, were looking to start a business resurfacing garage and basement cement floors with epoxy. I challenged them to clearly identify their target customer. Initially, they said, "Anyone who is frustrated with how their floor looks and wants a change." While this was true, they needed to dig deeper. Epoxy floor installation isn't simple; it requires specialized skills and knowledge to do it right. They realized that their unique skill set allowed them to offer a high-quality solution to homeowners looking for durable, attractive flooring.

One of their biggest advantages was the inherent trustworthiness they carried as first responders. Inviting someone into your home requires a level of trust that most strangers don't immediately inspire. As firefighters, Corbett and Joey already had that trust. People felt safe letting them into their homes, confident in their integrity and professionalism. In fact, some customers were so comfortable with them that they'd hand over their house keys and leave, knowing the job would be done right and their home respected. This level of trust, rooted in their reputation as firefighters, became a powerful asset that set them apart from other contractors.

Creating Customer Personas

Name: Lisa Thompson

Age: Forty-two

Occupation: Healthcare Administrator

Household Income: $120,000 annually

Location: Suburban residential neighborhood with mid to upper-middle-class homes.

Marital Status: Married with two children, ages nine and twelve.

Home Type: Single-family home with a two-car garage and a finished basement.

Primary Goals:

- Improve the appearance and functionality of her garage and basement floors.

- Find durable, attractive flooring that withstands wear and tear from kids, pets, and heavy use.
- Hire trustworthy professionals who will respect her home, family, and property.

Biggest Frustrations:

- Previous experiences with unreliable or unprofessional contractors.
- Fear of inviting strangers into her home when she is not there.
- Concern about poor workmanship that could lead to costly repairs down the line.

Values and Motivators:

- Strong values on safety, integrity, and professionalism.
- Prefers working with local businesses, especially those tied to trusted professions like firefighters and first responders.
- Willing to pay a premium for peace of mind and high-quality results.

Buying Decision Factors:

- Personal referrals from neighbors or friends.
- Positive online reviews and testimonials.
- Trust and professionalism displayed during the estimate and consultation process.
- Clear communication about the project timeline, costs, and expectations.

Why She Chooses Corbett and Joey:

- She feels an immediate sense of trust because they are firefighters, professionals who already serve her community.

- Their reputation for integrity and quality workmanship reassures her that the job will be done right without having to micromanage.
- Their ability to explain the technical process in clear, simple terms makes her feel informed and confident in her decision.

Developing Your Marketing Strategy

Your marketing strategy is the comprehensive plan you'll use to reach potential customers, build awareness, and generate interest in your business. It includes the tactics and channels you'll leverage to get your message out there and make meaningful connections with your target audience.

Content Marketing: Providing Value First

Content marketing is all about delivering valuable information that attracts and engages your audience. As a first responder, you have a wealth of knowledge that can be transformed into educational content— whether it's safety tips, expert insights, or behind-the-scenes looks at how your business operates.

Types of Content to Consider:

- **Blog Posts**: Write about topics relevant to your audience's pain points. For example, if you're in safety consulting, blog posts could cover "Top Ten Ways to Prepare Your Home for Emergencies" or "Why Fire Safety Drills Are Essential for Small Businesses."

- **Videos**: Videos can help humanize your brand and create a personal connection. You could share tutorials, safety demonstrations, or Q&A sessions. A simple video explaining "How to Perform Basic First Aid" could resonate with many.

- **Infographics**: Visual representations of important data or step-by-step guides can be highly shareable on social media.

- **Podcasts and Webinars**: Share your expertise through discussions or invite guests for a broader perspective. A podcast episode titled "Stories from the Field: Lessons Every Business Owner Can Learn from First Responders" could attract listeners interested in resilience and adaptability.

Practical Tip: Align your content calendar with seasonal or timely topics. For example, discuss winter safety tips before the colder months or fire safety tips before peak summer. In our business, we would host continuing education classes toward the end of the recertification cycle.

Real-Life Example: A fire safety business started by a retired firefighter shared weekly "Safety Saturday" tips on social media, building a loyal following and becoming the go-to expert for home safety advice.

Social Media Marketing: Connecting with Your Community

Social media platforms offer powerful opportunities to reach and engage with your target audience. Choose platforms that align with your business and audience demographics.

- **Facebook and Instagram**: Great for sharing visual content, behind-the-scenes posts, and community stories. Engage your followers by posting customer testimonials, live Q&A sessions, and interactive polls.

- **LinkedIn**: Ideal for B2B businesses and professional services. Share thought leadership articles and company updates, and engage in discussions relevant to your field.

- **Twitter (X)**: Useful for real-time updates, industry news, and brief tips. Engage with trending hashtags relevant to your field, like #FirstAid or #SafetyTips.

Best Practices for Social Media:

- Post consistently and maintain a schedule.
- Use high-quality images and videos. Ensure your photos or videos have your logo and branding embedded in them.

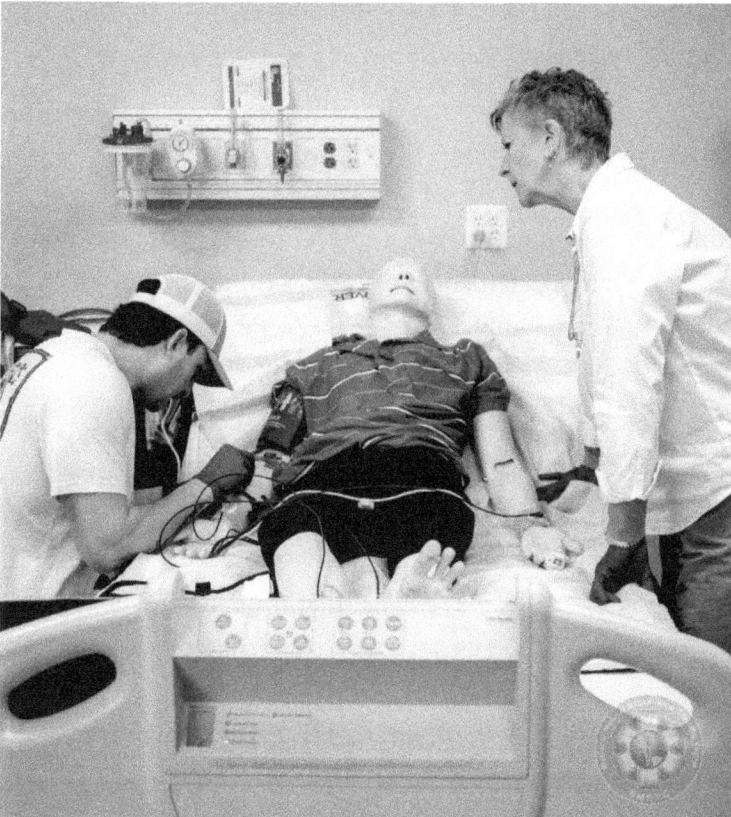

- Respond to comments and messages promptly to show you value customer interaction.
- Use stories and reels for quick, behind-the-scenes content or announcements.

PRO TIP: Use social media advertising to extend your reach.

Platforms like Facebook and Instagram allow you to create targeted ads based on demographics, interests, and behaviors, ensuring your message reaches the right people. In my experience, creating ads may require that you hire someone who has expertise navigating social media platforms and can optimize your ads as well as the money you spend on click-throughs. This could accelerate your learning curve and help you avoid wasting time and money.

Email Marketing: Staying Connected

Building an email list gives you a direct line of communication with your audience. Unlike social media, where algorithms dictate visibility, emails land directly in your subscribers' inboxes, making this channel a reliable way to maintain engagement.

Effective Email Marketing Strategies:

- **Welcome Series**: Introduce new subscribers to your brand with a series of welcome emails that highlight who you are, your mission, and what they can expect from your emails.

- **Educational Newsletters**: Share valuable insights, news, and tips that are relevant to your audience.

- **Exclusive Offers**: Reward your subscribers with special discounts, early access to products or services, and personalized content.

Personalization: Tailor your messages to different segments of your audience. For example, those who attended a webinar on "Home Fire Safety" could receive follow-up content related to that topic.

Case Study: Boosting Course Sign-Ups Through Strategic Follow-Ups

A safety training company saw a hefty thirty-five percent increase in course sign-ups simply by implementing a targeted follow-up email strategy. After hosting webinars, they sent personalized follow-up emails to attendees, offering exclusive discounts and providing additional resources related to the webinar topic.

The key to their success was timing and value. Each email was sent promptly after the webinar, ensuring the content was still fresh in the attendees' minds. The emails weren't just about selling; they included helpful resources, such as downloadable guides and links to relevant articles, which built trust and reinforced the company's expertise.

At the end of each email, they made a clear and compelling offer for attendees to enroll in their courses, creating a sense of urgency with limited-time discounts or bonuses for signing up early.

Lesson: Boldness Drives Results

This case study highlights the importance of boldness in business. Don't hesitate to make an offer, and be confident in the value of your product or service. Success often favors those willing to take calculated risks and make their pitch. By adding value and following up strategically, you can turn potential leads into loyal customers.

Search Engine Optimization (SEO): Boosting Your Visibility

SEO is crucial for increasing your website's visibility in search engine results. By optimizing your website for relevant keywords and ensuring it's user-friendly, you make it easier for potential customers to find you. Engage your web developer in adding SEO to your website. The following are some of the techniques they're likely to employ.

Key SEO Techniques:

- **Keyword Research**: Identify keywords and phrases that potential customers might use to search for your products or services. Tools like Google Keyword Planner or SEMrush can help.

- **On-Page Optimization**: Incorporate relevant keywords into your website's content in a natural, organic way, including titles, headers, and meta descriptions.

- **High-Quality Content**: Search engines favor websites that provide valuable, original content. Regularly updating your site with informative blog posts and guides can improve your rankings.

- **Mobile Optimization**: Ensure your website is mobile-friendly, as a significant portion of web traffic comes from mobile devices.

Example: A small business providing CPR training optimized their site with keywords like "CPR certification near me" and "online CPR courses." This strategic use of SEO led to a fifty percent increase in organic traffic within six months.

I strongly recommend taking time to familiarize yourself with the basic terminology and principles of SEO, or Search Engine Optimization. Understanding even the fundamentals will help you have more informed conversations with your website developer or an SEO specialist. I cannot stress enough how critical it is to work with someone who truly understands the art and science of SEO. You can build a beautiful website, but if it is not optimized correctly, it will remain virtually invisible to the people you want to reach. SEO is what makes your website findable when someone types in keywords related to your business.

At NMETC, we learned this lesson early on. In the beginning, we built a strong website, but what really accelerated our reach was investing in strategic SEO. We worked closely with experts who knew how to optimize our pages, content, and structure around the keywords and search behaviors of prospective students. Because of that, NMETC consistently shows up on the first page of major search engines when students search for online paramedic programs or EMS education. This visibility has had a direct and profound impact on our growth.

If you are serious about expanding your business, investing in SEO is not optional, it is essential. A great product or service deserves to be seen, and SEO is how you make sure it is.

Building Relationships and Networking

As a first responder, you know that trust and strong relationships are vital. In business, building relationships is just as important, especially when it comes to sales. Networking, both online and in-person, allows you to connect with potential customers, partners, and industry influencers who can help grow your business.

Attending Industry Events

Conferences, trade shows, and networking events offer opportunities to meet potential customers and partners face-to-face. Your presence in these spaces increases visibility and allows for meaningful interactions.

Tips for Successful Networking:

- Prepare an elevator pitch that succinctly explains who you are and what you offer.

- Bring business cards or digital contact options to share with new connections.

- Follow up with people you meet—send a quick email or LinkedIn message to keep the connection warm.

Case Study: The Power of Networking at EMS World Conference:

Walking through the vendor area at the EMS World Conference, I felt the familiar buzz of my phone. It was a notification from Facebook Messenger, a message from an EMT in Iceland named Ivar. He was inquiring about our paramedic program. Intrigued, I clicked on his profile to learn more about him and his department.

As I scanned his profile picture and looked back up, I noticed a small group of people standing at a nearby vendor booth. I glanced down at my phone, then back up at the group. I couldn't believe it: there he was, standing right in front of me. It felt like one of those serendipitous moments you couldn't plan if you tried.

I called out, "Ivar!" He turned around, equally surprised and slightly confused. We both realized what had just happened, a message sent minutes earlier had led to a face-to-face introduction. We shook hands, and I introduced myself to him and the group he was with. They were equally astonished at the timing and connection.

Ivar explained that he had heard about our paramedic program from another attendee, who'd encouraged him to reach out to me for more information. Neither of them had any idea that I was also at the conference. What followed was an impromptu discussion about our program. I launched into my elevator pitch, sharing the value and structure of our paramedic training. Their interest was immediate—they were hooked, and began asking questions about how the program could work for them.

Digital Networking in Action

Whether it's Facebook Messenger or some other digital platform, it helped us make a connection that led to a face-to-face interaction in just minutes. I shared my details with Ivar instantly, and he reciprocated by providing his. I promised to follow up with more details that evening. Today, I not only use traditional business cards, but also have a dot.card: a single card that can be tapped to most smartphones and transfer all my contact information to the person I just met without worrying about losing a business card. It also has a QR code that can be scanned to take you to the online dot.card information.

Back at my hotel room that night, I composed personalized follow-up emails to each of them, thanking them for the conversation and providing additional information about our program. The follow-up wasn't just a formality, it reinforced the connection we'd made earlier and kept the momentum going.

The Results

That single interaction led to all members of the group enrolling in our online paramedic program. Each enrollment represented about $10,000 in revenue, resulting in over $50,000 from just one chance meeting. But the impact of attending the EMS World Conference didn't stop there. Over the course of the event, I spoke with numerous other attendees and connected with many who later signed up for our program. By the time the conference ended, the total revenue generated from these interactions exceeded $150,000.

The cost to attend the conference, including flights, hotel, and entrance fees, was approximately $3,000. The return on investment (ROI) was staggering. That $3,000 investment not only generated significant revenue but also expanded our program's reach to an entirely new market in Iceland. Since that interaction, we have had many Icelandic students attend our paramedic program.

Lessons Learned

This experience reinforced several key principles of networking and the value of industry events:

1. **Be Prepared for Opportunity**: Always be ready to pitch your product or service, even in unexpected moments. Opportunities can arise anywhere, and being prepared can make all the difference.

2. **Leverage Technology**: Digital tools like dot.cards or other contact-sharing platforms can make networking seamless and efficient. They're especially useful for international connections or tech-savvy professionals. Smartphones also allow you to share your contact information as well.

3. **Follow-Up Is Crucial**: Networking doesn't end with an introduction. Following up promptly and thoughtfully can turn a casual conversation into a lasting relationship—and substantial revenue, as in this case.

4. **ROI Matters**: Attending conferences and industry events can feel like an expense, but when done strategically, the ROI can far outweigh the costs. Beyond direct sales, these events build brand awareness and foster connections that pay dividends over time.

5. **Personal Connections Are Powerful**: In a digital age, face-to-face interactions still hold immense value. Meeting Ivar and his team in person created a level of trust and connection that wouldn't have been possible through email or social media alone.

Networking isn't just about handing out business cards or attending events—it's about building authentic connections and seizing opportunities as they arise. That single message on Facebook Messenger turned into a chance meeting, which led to expanding our program internationally, building lasting relationships, and achieving incredible ROI. We now have over fifty students from Iceland. It's a testament to the power of being present, prepared, and proactive in every interaction.

Leveraging Online Communities

Engage in online forums, Facebook groups, LinkedIn groups, and other digital communities where your target audience or industry peers are active. Contribute to discussions, offer advice, and share your expertise to build trust and establish yourself as a thought leader.

Collaborating with Other Businesses

Creating strategic partnerships with complementary businesses can expand your reach and attract new customers. For example, if you run a safety consulting firm, consider collaborating with local hardware stores or fire equipment suppliers to cross-promote services. In my business, we created several strategic partnerships that not only helped us expand our offerings to our students, but also increased sales for our strategic partner. One particular example was, we had a great strategic partnership with a continuing education company. I would buy the content from our partner at a big discount, we would add value to the content and resell it to our customers. It created new customers for our partner, and we were able to buy content cheaply and upsell it to our customers, creating a win–win.

PRO TIP: Look for win–win collaborations. Both businesses should benefit from the partnership to create a lasting, productive relationship.

Sales Strategies: Turning Leads into Customers

Your marketing efforts are designed to generate interest and leads. Now, it's time to convert that interest into sales. While the world of sales can seem far removed from the life of a first responder, many of the same skills apply: clear communication, active listening, and problem-solving under pressure.

Understanding the Customer's Needs

The best salespeople are great listeners. Taking the time to understand your customer's needs and concerns is essential. Ask questions and pay attention to their answers. When you truly understand their pain points, you can tailor your pitch to show how your product or service solves their problem.

Example Questions to Ask:

- What challenges are you currently facing?
- What solutions have you tried before, and why didn't they work?
- What are your main priorities when choosing a service or product?

Building Trust

Trust is the foundation of any successful sale. Be transparent, honest, and reliable in all your communications. If you don't have an immediate answer to a question, admit it and commit to finding out. This authenticity can go a long way in establishing a positive relationship.

Case Study: Building Trust Through Transparency

A small business specializing in emergency preparedness kits experienced remarkable success by adopting a transparent and customer-focused approach. Instead of merely emphasizing the strengths of their products, they openly discussed their kits' limitations and offered tailored solutions to address individual customer needs. This strategy not only built trust but also positioned the company as a reliable and empathetic resource in their market.

The Challenge

Many emergency preparedness kit providers focus solely on promoting their products' strengths, often overlooking the diverse needs of their customers. This small business recognized that a one-size-fits-all approach wasn't enough, as every household, workplace, or community has unique requirements. Customers often had concerns about how well a standard kit would meet their specific situations, such as accommodating a family with young children, someone with medical conditions, or employees in high-risk industries.

The Strategy

The company pivoted from a generic sales pitch to a consultative, transparent approach:

1. **Acknowledging Limitations:** When engaging with customers, they openly discussed the limitations of their standard kits, such as lacking certain medical supplies or enough provisions for larger families. Instead of trying to upsell unnecessarily, they focused on ensuring the customer felt informed and understood.

2. **Offering Tailored Solutions:** They provided options for customizing kits to meet specific needs. For example, they recommended adding infant care items for families with young children or extra medication storage for individuals with chronic health conditions.

3. **Educational Content:** The business created educational content, such as blog posts, videos, and webinars, explaining how to assess preparedness needs and identify potential gaps. This not only added value but also positioned them as a trusted authority in emergency preparedness.

The Results

1. **Increased Customer Trust:** By addressing limitations honestly, customers felt the company genuinely cared about their well-being rather than just making a sale. This transparency fostered strong relationships and built brand loyalty.

2. **Repeat Business:** Many customers returned to purchase additional supplies or updated kits as their circumstances changed, knowing they could rely on the company's expertise and integrity.

3. **Word-of-Mouth Referrals:** Satisfied customers frequently recommended the business to friends, family, and colleagues, leading to a steady stream of new clients. Customers highlighted the company's honesty and personalized service as key reasons for their referrals.

4. **Revenue Growth:** Despite the initial focus on limitations, the approach resulted in an upswing in sales as customers added tailored items to their orders, driving higher average order values.

KEY TAKEAWAYS:

1. **Honesty Builds Loyalty:** Customers appreciate businesses that prioritize their needs over a quick sale. Transparency fosters trust, which translates into repeat business and referrals.

2. **Customization Drives Value:** Offering tailored solutions allows you to meet customer-specific needs, setting your business apart from competitors who rely on generic offerings.

3. **Educational Engagement Pays Off:** Sharing knowledge demonstrates your expertise and creates a sense of partnership with your customers, encouraging long-term loyalty.

By prioritizing trust and focusing on tailored solutions, this small business not only strengthened its reputation but also achieved sustainable growth, proving that honesty truly is the best policy in customer relations.

Focusing on Value, Not Just Features

Rather than focusing solely on the features of your product or service, highlight the value it provides to the customer. How does it make their life easier? What specific problems does it solve? By focusing on benefits, you create a stronger emotional connection.

Example: If you're selling an online CPR course, don't just list the modules included. Emphasize how taking the course could help someone save a loved one's life.

Following Up

Many sales are lost simply due to a lack of follow-up. After an initial conversation or presentation, it's crucial to check in with your prospects. A simple follow-up email or call can remind them of your offer and address any lingering questions. Successful salespeople often follow up with a prospect seven to fifteen times before closing the deal. That takes real dedication and persistence. Remember, most people won't make a purchasing decision after the first interaction. While there will always be early adopters willing to take that initial leap with you, they are few and far between. The majority will need constant reassurance that your product or service is legitimate and truly meets their needs. This process of persistent follow-up is essential to build trust and move your prospects from interest to commitment.

PRO TIP: Utilize CRM (customer relationship management) software to manage interactions and schedule follow-ups effectively.

With numerous CRM options available, it's important to select one that is user-friendly and suits your business needs. In my business, we've optimized our process so that all leads flow automatically from our website into our CRM. This type of automation saves valuable time and ensures that no lead falls through the cracks.

Choose a CRM that complements your workflow and supports automated responses and follow-ups. For example, our website is designed so that when a student submits an application for one of our programs, their information is seamlessly entered into our CRM. The system then assigns a task to our administrative team to review the application and follow the next steps. Incorporating these automations creates a seamless experience for both the business and the customer, enhancing efficiency and ensuring consistent follow-up.

Tracking and Measuring Your Success

It's essential to track and measure your marketing and sales efforts to understand what's working and what needs adjustment. Use analytics tools like Google Analytics, social media insights, and email marketing metrics to gather data on your campaigns.

Key Metrics to Monitor:

- **Website Traffic**: Where are your visitors coming from, and which pages are they visiting most?

- **Conversion Rates**: How many leads turn into paying customers?

- **Engagement**: How many likes, shares, and comments do your social media posts receive?

- **Open and Click-Through Rates**: How often are your marketing emails opened, and how many recipients click on the links?

By regularly reviewing these metrics, you can refine your marketing and sales strategies, focusing on what delivers the best results.

Chapter Thoughts

Marketing and sales are critical components of growing your business. As a first responder, you already possess the discipline, resilience, and communication skills needed to succeed in these areas. By understanding your audience, developing a robust marketing strategy, building meaningful relationships, and refining your sales techniques, you'll be well on your way to attracting and retaining customers.

In the next chapter, we'll explore resource management: how to manage your time, finances, and personnel effectively to ensure your business runs smoothly and efficiently. Let's keep moving forward on your entrepreneurial journey. You've built a strong foundation, now it's time to start seeing the results.

CHAPTER 7

Managing Resources—Time, Money, and People

As a first responder, you know firsthand that resource management can mean the difference between a successful operation and one that falls apart under pressure. Whether it's deploying personnel effectively or ensuring an operation runs smoothly with limited resources, these principles are just as vital when managing a business. The challenge lies in translating the skills and instincts that come naturally to you on the job into managing your business resources—time, finances, and people. In this chapter, we'll explore comprehensive strategies to help you manage these critical areas and create a thriving business that aligns with your life as a first responder.

Time Management: Juggling Two Roles

One of the biggest challenges of being a first responder-entrepreneur is effectively managing your time. Balancing the demands of your job, your family, and your business requires not only discipline but also a strategic approach to time management. Unlike typical entrepreneurs, your role as a first responder comes with unpredictable shifts and duties, which means you need to be adaptable while staying organized and focused.

Understanding the Value of Time

The saying "time is money" is especially true for entrepreneurs. How you manage your time can directly impact your productivity and the success of your business. The goal is to work not just harder but smarter. This means focusing your time and energy on tasks that yield the greatest return.

PRO TIP: Think of your time as an investment. Every hour you spend should contribute to growth and sustainability for you personally, professionally, and in your business.

Strategies for Optimizing Your Time

Prioritize Tasks: Start by identifying your top priorities for the day, week, or month. Whether it's completing a major project for your business or preparing for an important training session at work, knowing what needs the most attention allows you to allocate your energy effectively. The Eisenhower Matrix can be particularly helpful. Developed by President Dwight D. Eisenhower and popularized by productivity experts, this matrix helps you organize tasks and decisions by urgency and importance. It's based on the evaluation of the importance and urgency of tasks. An urgent task is one that needs to be completed by a specific time; an important task is one with significant repercussions. Not all urgent tasks are important, and not all important tasks are urgent. By working out which are which, you can allocate the time required for them more effectively.

IMPORTANT

URGENT & IMPORTANT DO Crisis, Deadlines	NOT URGENT & IMPORTANT SCHEDULE Planning, Exercise
URGENT & NOT IMPORTANT DELEGATE Interruptions, Meetings	NOT URGENT & NOT IMPORTANT ELIMINATE Time Wasters, Distractions

URGENT

NOT URGENT

NOT IMPORTANT

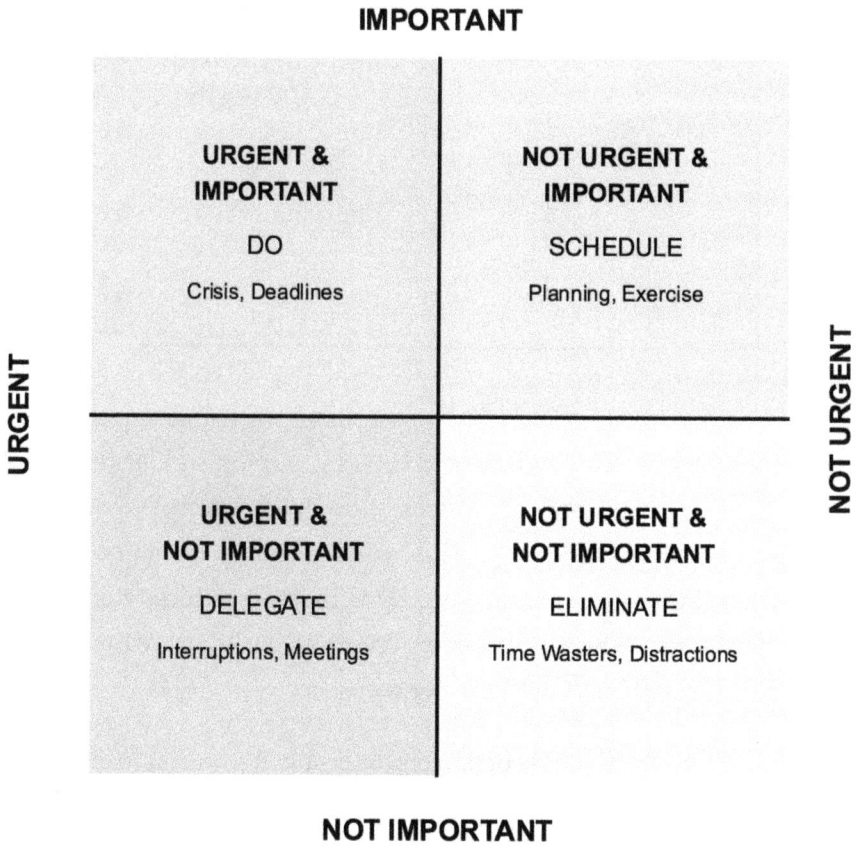

Time-Blocking: Allocate specific time slots for different activities and commit to them as if they were non-negotiable appointments. For example, dedicate a couple of hours before or after your shifts to focus solely on business tasks. Time-blocking ensures that you maintain a balance between your daily responsibilities and your entrepreneurial goals.

Daily Time Blocking Schedule

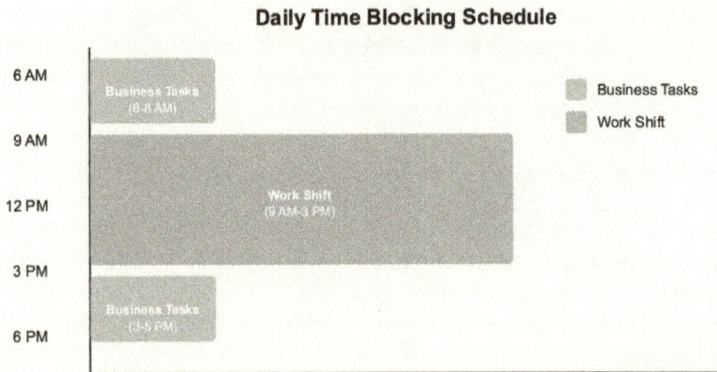

Batch Processing: Batch processing involves grouping similar tasks and tackling them during a dedicated block of time. For example, you might set aside an hour to respond to emails, schedule social media posts, and update your CRM system all at once. This method reduces the mental load of constantly switching between unrelated tasks, allowing you to work more efficiently and with greater focus.

To maximize the effectiveness of batch processing, it's crucial to eliminate distractions. When I need to focus and complete tasks efficiently, one of my go-to strategies is putting my iPhone on "Focus" mode. Since I use Mac devices across my workflow (MacBook, iPad, and iPhone), this feature syncs seamlessly across all of them, muting incoming messages and notifications. This eliminates interruptions like the buzz of my Apple Watch or a flood of alerts popping up on my screens.

I am connected to several breaking news networks, including a group called TAC-9. This is a group of first responders, dispatchers, and lay people who listen to local departments and text out to the group when fires or other serious incidents are happening in my area. I love to stay informed as to what is happening around me. However, the information flow coming from this group can be overwhelming when lots of serious incidents are happening. At times, I need to shut them off, or I would never get anything done. (But when you tune the rest of the world out, be sure that your family can still get through to you!)

Without this safeguard, it's easy to get derailed by constant notifications, pulling my attention away from the task at hand. Research shows that even brief distractions can disrupt your concentration. According to Gloria Mark's work at the University of California, it takes about twenty-five minutes on average to regain your focus. By using Focus mode or similar features on other devices, you create a distraction-free environment that allows you to stay fully immersed in your work.

Delegate and Outsource: One of the most important lessons in entrepreneurship is recognizing that you can't, and shouldn't, do everything on your own. Delegating tasks to employees or outsourcing certain functions, such as administrative work, marketing, or bookkeeping, is not just about freeing up time—it's about aligning your efforts with your highest priorities. As Dan Martell emphasizes in his book *Buy Back Your Time*, the key to effective entrepreneurship is learning to identify tasks that represent an unproductive use of your time and energy or fall outside your expertise, and entrusting them to others. This strategic delegation not only frees you from the grind of low-value activities but also empowers you to focus on high-impact efforts that drive growth, foster innovation, and ensure the long-term success of your business. By buying back your time, you're investing in the areas where your unique skills and vision can truly make a difference.

For early-stage entrepreneurs, this can feel like a daunting step. You might think, *I can't afford to hire help yet,* or, *No one can do this as well as I can.* But the reality is, there are cost-effective ways to delegate even as a one-person startup. Platforms like Upwork, Fiverr, and Toptal provide access to skilled freelancers who can take tasks off your plate at a fraction of the cost of hiring full-time staff.

Prioritizing Your Role: What Should You Not Be Doing?

As your business begins to grow, one of the most important questions you can ask yourself as a leader is this: *What should I no longer be doing at my level of the organization?* This simple question can help you shift your mindset from doer to builder, from someone in the trenches doing every task, to someone who is leading with vision and creating space for others to succeed. I also use this exercise and ask key leaders in my business the same question. It helps them understand the tasks they are doing that they should not be doing.

This concept is echoed by business coach and author Dan Martell in his book *Buy Back Your Time.* He poses another powerful question: "What is your time worth?" It's not just a motivational line, it's a tool to help you understand the real value of your time and energy. Martell encourages entrepreneurs to calculate their effective hourly rate by combining all forms of compensation, salary, distributions, and profit, and dividing that by the number of hours they work in a week.

Let's say you make $250,000 annually from your business. Divided by 52 weeks, that's about $4,800 per week. Divide that by 40 hours, and you're looking at an hourly rate of $120. Now ask yourself: *Are you spending hours each week on $25-per-hour tasks like managing your inbox, scheduling meetings, or updating spreadsheets?* Because if you are, you're leaving high-value work on the table, the kind of work only you, as the visionary and leader of the business, can do.

These are the moments when delegation becomes not just a nice-to-have but a must. Strategic thinking, big-picture planning, partnerships, and growth decisions are the places where your time and energy yield the highest return. Everything else can (and should) be handed off, either to team members or outsourced professionals.

I had this epiphany long before Martell's book came out. I was driving on the highway listening to a completely unrelated podcast. My mind started drifting, and I thought about a problem we had in our clinical team. My Director of Clinical Services was task-saturated, and I thought about the things she was doing. It was then that I asked what she was doing every day that she should not be doing at her level of the organization. Then, as I thought about this, I started thinking about all the leaders, myself included.

This shift in mindset was a game-changer for me. Once I began to truly understand where my key leaders and I created the most value in our business, we started letting go of the rest, and that's when our growth really accelerated.

Remember, great leaders don't do everything. They focus on their strengths and build teams to do the rest.

Practical Steps to Delegation and Outsourcing

1. **Identify Tasks to Delegate or Outsource:**

   o List all your daily, weekly, and monthly tasks.

   o Highlight tasks that are repetitive, time-consuming, or outside your expertise. Common examples include bookkeeping, data entry, graphic design, email marketing, or IT support.

2. **Determine the Return on Investment (ROI) of Delegation:**

   o Estimate how much time these tasks take and compare the cost of outsourcing them versus doing them yourself at your hourly rate.

o   Example: If you're spending 5 hours a week on bookkeeping and your hourly value is $120, that's $600 of your time. Hiring a freelance bookkeeper for $150 a week saves you $450 and allows you to redirect those hours toward growth-focused activities.

3. **Leverage Technology and Platforms:**

o   Use platforms like **Upwork** or **Fiverr** to find skilled freelancers for specific tasks.

o   For administrative help, consider **virtual assistants** through platforms like **Belay** or **Zirtual**.

o   For bookkeeping, tools like **QuickBooks Live** or outsourcing to small firms can simplify your financial management.

4. **Set Clear Expectations:**

o   Clearly outline the scope of work, deadlines, and deliverables for any outsourced task.

o   Regularly communicate and provide feedback to ensure quality and alignment with your business goals.

Delegation in Action: My Experience

As our organization began to grow, I found myself stuck in the day-to-day grind, buried in tasks that didn't align with my role as a leader. I was juggling everything from creating slide decks to managing schedules, and while it felt like I was working hard, I wasn't working smart. The bigger picture was getting lost. I was so caught up in the operations that I wasn't leading us toward the next level of growth.

That's when I started asking a different question. Instead of asking what else I had to do, I asked, *Where should I be spending my time to most effectively lead and grow this business?* That one question opened my eyes. I realized that the way I was operating was capping our potential. I was not only wasting time on tasks that others could handle, but I was limiting our organization's ability to expand.

John Maxwell's "Law of the Lid" says that leadership ability is the lid that determines a person's level of effectiveness. The organization cannot rise above the level of its leader. That truth hit me hard. I knew that if I wanted our business to grow, I had to grow first. I had to learn to let go, to delegate, to trust others with responsibilities that were no longer the best use of my time. If I didn't raise my lid as a leader, I was going to be the reason we stalled.

So I started with something simple. I outsourced our bookkeeping to a small firm. It immediately freed up hours each week. Hours I could now dedicate to thinking strategically, building partnerships, and focusing on how to scale. That one move gave me room to breathe. Next, I hired a virtual assistant to manage the administrative work tied to our educational programs. Scheduling, documentation, emails, all of it was now in the hands of someone who excelled in that space.

The impact was immediate. Tasks that once felt like a weight on my shoulders were now off my plate and getting done better than I ever did them. It wasn't just a matter of time saved; it was about energy and focus. Those low-value tasks had been draining me. They took time away from the work that energized me, the work that only I could do, to move our business forward. Delegating gave me back that capacity.

This shift changed everything. It wasn't just about being more efficient. It was about growing into the leader my team, and my company needed me to be. I began to spend my time where it mattered most, where I could actually make a difference. The moment I made that shift, the growth came faster. Our team functioned better, our systems improved, and we were finally able to scale in a sustainable way.

What I learned is this: being a leader does not mean doing everything. It means doing the right things and empowering others to do the rest. If you want your business to grow, you have to grow first. Raise your lid, step into your role as a leader, and trust your team to rise with you. That is how real progress begins.

KEY TAKEAWAY: Delegation isn't just a luxury; it's a necessity for growth. By outsourcing tasks that don't require your direct involvement, you create space to focus on what you do best, whether it's leading your team, innovating, or driving revenue. Start small, use cost-effective resources, and build a delegation strategy that grows alongside your business.

Remember, your time is your most valuable asset. Invest it wisely!

I learned early on that delegation isn't just about handing off tasks; it's about equipping people with the knowledge, support, and trust they need to succeed. In the beginning, you can't simply assign a responsibility and walk away. You have to teach into it. That means providing clear guidance, setting expectations, and checking in to ensure that tasks are being executed the way you envisioned. However—and this is key—**be open to change**. The way you've always done things may not be the best way, and if you've hired someone with expertise in a particular area, you need to give them the freedom to improve the process. True delegation isn't about micromanagement; it's about empowering people to take ownership.

As the business grew, I found myself doing this repeatedly, to the point where delegation became second nature. The ability to hand off responsibilities confidently was a game-changer, not just for efficiency, but for the long-term success of the organization. Scaling a business means building a team that can operate without you being involved in every single detail.

I saw striking similarities between this and my first promotion to lieutenant in the fire department. I went from being a task-level firefighter—grabbing the nozzle, forcing the door, stretching hose—to leading an entire engine company. My role shifted. While I still needed to be technically proficient in all the hands-on aspects of the job, it was no longer *my* job to be the one putting water on the fire. Instead, I had to step back, conduct a size-up, determine which hose line we needed, direct my firefighters to their assignments, lead them into the structure, ensure the building was searched for victims, and make sure water was applied effectively to extinguish the fire. Most importantly, I was responsible for their safety and the safety of those around them.

The transition from *doing* to *leading* is a challenge many first responders face when stepping into leadership roles, and the same is true in business. At first, you may feel the pull to jump in and do everything yourself because that's what you've always done. But leadership, whether in the firehouse or in your business, demands that you trust your people to execute, support them as they develop, and give them the authority to take ownership. That's how teams grow. That's how businesses scale. And that's how you, as a leader, evolve from being just a high-performing individual to someone who builds a high-performing organization.

Leverage Technology: Use technology to automate and streamline processes. Project management tools like Trello, Asana, or Monday.com can help you organize tasks and deadlines, while scheduling apps can ensure you're making the most of your limited time. Automating routine tasks such as email follow-ups, invoice reminders, or social media posts can save you hours each week.

Real-Life Example: One first responder entrepreneur used a combination of Google Calendar and Trello to map out daily tasks and long-term goals. By setting recurring tasks for administrative duties and customer follow-ups, they kept their business organized while managing the unpredictable nature of their first responder shifts.

Stay Organized: Maintaining a well-organized workspace and schedule helps reduce stress and improve productivity. Whether you prefer a physical planner, a digital tool, or a combination of both, having a system in place to track tasks, deadlines, and goals is essential for staying on top of your workload. I personally am a tech kind of guy. Using digital tools helps sync my calendar instantly across all my devices (I use five devices on a regular basis). As our organization grew, we switched from all paper records to all digital. I want to be anywhere in the world, and as long as I have a computer and internet access, I have instant information about our business at my fingertips. This also helped when I was on shift and needed something to answer a question or take care of a problem.

PRO TIP: At the end of each week, spend fifteen minutes planning the week ahead.

This practice can help you identify your priorities and mentally prepare for what's to come. I personally do this Sunday night. It's my time to reflect on the week and set the priorities for the week ahead. This keeps me focused on what is important in my business and what needs my attention. I review my SMART goals and ensure I am moving toward them. I will lay out my calendar and set reminders, as well as block time for tasks that will help move the business forward. Create a work environment in your home, whether it's a home office or just a quiet place somewhere in your house where you have space to think and work

Balancing Work and Business

Finding balance is often the hardest part of managing dual roles. Here are some additional strategies:

- **Set Realistic Goals**: It's easy to overestimate what you can accomplish in a day and underestimate what you can achieve in a year. Break down larger business goals into manageable daily or weekly tasks. This will keep you moving forward without overwhelming you.

- **Create Boundaries**: Establishing clear boundaries is essential to balancing your responsibilities as a first responder and an entrepreneur. Without defined limits, it's easy for the demands of one role to spill over into the other, causing stress and anxiety, and reducing your effectiveness in both areas. Setting boundaries helps you stay focused, maintain productivity, and ensure you're fully present in each role.

Define Work Hours for Each Role

Start by carving out dedicated time for your business and your first responder duties. Be realistic about your availability and create a schedule that reflects your priorities. Clearly communicate this schedule with family, colleagues, and staff to avoid misunderstandings. Transparency ensures that everyone knows when you're focused on one role and unavailable for the other.

Leverage Tools to Communicate Boundaries

Use tools like shared calendars or scheduling apps to block off time for your first responder shifts and business tasks. My staff has my firehouse schedule uploaded into our school calendar. They know when I'm on duty and understand not to contact me unless it's a true emergency. This system removes ambiguity and allows my team to manage most issues independently while respecting my firehouse responsibilities.

Educate Your Team on Your Roles

Help your team understand the unique demands of your first responder role. As a shift commander, I'm responsible not only for responding to emergencies but also for managing the daily operations of my shift. My staff knows this requires my full attention, and I trust their judgment about what constitutes an emergency that requires my input.

Establishing Emergency Protocols: Empowering Your Team to Act

Every business encounters unexpected challenges. As an entrepreneur, you cannot always be the one to solve them in real time. That is why it is essential to establish clear emergency protocols. Your team needs to know what qualifies as a true emergency, how to handle day-to-day issues independently, and when it is necessary to escalate something to you. By defining these protocols, you create a structured approach that ensures your business runs smoothly even when you are not immediately available.

One of the most powerful ways to support your team is by giving them the tools and authority to solve problems on their own. In my company, I have provided key leaders with business credit cards and the autonomy to make financial decisions when necessary. But it goes beyond just having access to money. It's about fostering a culture of trust and empowerment.

A perfect example of this happened when one of our students, who had traveled from across the country to attend our program, found herself stranded in Boston, thirty miles from the hotel. She had lost her wallet at the airport before departing from her home city. When she landed in Boston, she realized she had no access to money.

In a panic, she reported her cards stolen and had them shut down, but then realized too late that she had already linked her card to her Uber app and could have still used it. Now stranded, unable to check into her hotel without a credit card, and with no cash for food, she was stuck.

She called our office, frantic. Because we had an empowered team with clear protocols in place, our staff immediately stepped in. They booked her an Uber to get her safely to the hotel, contacted the front desk, and used our company credit card to secure her room. The next morning, our COO personally handed her cash so she could buy food while waiting for her bank to send a replacement debit card.

This could have been a nightmare scenario for the student: alone in a new city, financially stranded, unsure of what to do. But because our team had the resources and authority to act, they transformed a crisis into a customer service win. The student later told us she had never felt so supported by an educational institution before, and this experience solidified her trust in us.

This is why empowering your team is critical. Emergencies happen, whether it's a logistical issue, a customer in distress, or a last-minute operational hurdle. If your team knows they have both the permission and the resources to act, they will step up. That is leadership. That is how you build a company that can function and thrive beyond your personal involvement.

The lesson is simple: do not just prepare for emergencies, prepare your team to handle them. Provide clear decision-making authority, equip them with the necessary resources, and instill a culture of problem-solving. When your people feel trusted and empowered, they will take ownership and ensure that challenges do not turn into disasters, but rather become opportunities to build even stronger relationships with your customers.

Communicate with Family and Friends

Balancing two demanding roles often means your personal time is limited. Share your schedule with your family and close friends so they understand when you're working and when you're available to spend time with them. By setting expectations early, you reduce the risk of disappointment or conflict.

Utilize Downtime Wisely

Take advantage of quieter periods during shifts, such as breaks or downtime, to tackle small business tasks such as responding to emails or brainstorming new ideas. Ensure that this is permitted and doesn't interfere with your primary responsibilities as a first responder. Personally, I made it a habit to avoid the "Lifesucker 2000" at the firehouse (a.k.a. the recliner). Instead, I used my time purposefully. Once all station duties, training, and administrative tasks were complete, I dedicated my downtime between calls to planning and preparing for my upcoming days off. I also focused on personal development to enhance my skills, ensuring I could grow both as a leader and in my business.

Developing myself was essential not just for my growth but to effectively lead and expand my business team. I had to grow myself so I could grow those around me!

Financial Management: Keeping Your Business on Solid Ground

Financial management is one of the most crucial elements of running a successful business. As a first responder, you're accustomed to working with limited resources and making critical decisions under pressure, skills that can be leveraged when handling your business finances.

Creating a Budget: Your Financial Blueprint

A comprehensive budget is the foundation of financial health. Your budget should outline all your expected income and expenses, covering everything from startup costs and operational expenses to marketing and payroll.

Steps to Create an Effective Budget:

1. **List Fixed and Variable Expenses**: Fixed expenses are regular and predictable, such as rent, insurance, and software subscriptions. Variable expenses include marketing, raw materials, or contractor fees.

2. **Include Contingencies**: Set aside a portion of your budget for unexpected expenses. Just as you prepare for unforeseen emergencies on the job, financial preparedness in business can mean the difference between stability and crisis.

3. **Project Revenue**: Be realistic but optimistic in your revenue projections. Consider seasonal trends or external factors that might affect your sales.

> **PRO TIP**: Review your budget monthly to ensure you're staying on track, and make adjustments as needed.

As my business expanded, I eventually hired an external accounting firm (AccountingDepartment.com) to handle our financial reporting. This remote firm manages our bookkeeping and comprehensive financial tracking. Each month, they provide me with a Profit and Loss (P&L) report, a Balance Sheet, and a Cash Flow statement.

Every December, I meet with their team to create a budget for the upcoming year. My monthly P&L report is then compared against our budgeted revenue and expenses. This practice gives me a clear and consistent overview of where our organization stands financially each month. As a business owner, understanding your numbers is crucial. While you may not need this level of support in the startup phase, I highly recommend outsourcing financial management as your business becomes more complex. If I could offer one piece of advice as your company grows, it would be to prioritize outsourcing payroll and accounting as soon as you can afford it. These areas are essential for maintaining financial accuracy and allowing you to focus on growing your business.

Separating Business and Personal Finances

Maintaining a clear boundary between your business and personal finances is essential. Open a dedicated business bank account and use it exclusively for all business transactions. This separation not only simplifies accounting but also provides legal protection for your personal assets.

Managing Financial Records with Tools That Fit Your Needs

Accurate financial records are essential for any business. Tools like QuickBooks or Wave can streamline the process by tracking income and expenses and generating detailed reports, making tax preparation significantly easier.

Start Simple: Use Spreadsheets in the Beginning

In the early stages of your business, you don't need to jump straight into complex accounting software. A simple Excel spreadsheet or Apple Numbers file can work perfectly well for tracking income and expenses. There are numerous free templates available online that can help you create basic financial tracking systems, allowing you to manage your records with minimal setup or learning curve. This simple system helps you track money in and money out!

Know When to Delegate

I learned the hard way that trying to force myself to master accounting software wasn't the best use of my time. Early in my business journey, I struggled with QuickBooks because I didn't fully understand the terminology or structure of accounting. I spent hours wrestling with concepts like a "Chart of Accounts," only to realize I was in over my head. The frustration was real, and I knew I needed help.

That's when I applied the advice from Dan Sullivan's book *Who Not How*. The premise is simple: instead of asking, "How can I figure this out?" ask, "Who can help me with this?" This shift in mindset was a game-changer for me. I realized that learning the intricacies of accounting software wasn't the best use of my time as a business owner. My role was to grow the business, not to become a bookkeeper.

Hire a Bookkeeper When You're Ready

If managing your financial records becomes too complex or time-consuming, hiring a professional bookkeeper can be one of the best investments you make. A skilled bookkeeper can take over tasks like categorizing expenses, reconciling accounts, and preparing financial reports, freeing you to focus on growing your business. They can also provide insights into your finances, helping you make more informed decisions.

Transition to Advanced Tools as You Grow

As your business expands, you may reach a point where more advanced accounting tools are necessary. At that stage, a professional bookkeeper or accountant can help you set up the software correctly and teach you how to interpret the reports it generates. With the right support, transitioning to tools like QuickBooks becomes a smoother and more valuable process.

KEY TAKEAWAY: Your time as a business owner is best spent on high-impact activities that align with your strengths. If accounting isn't one of them, start simple with spreadsheets and seek help when needed. Whether it's hiring a bookkeeper or eventually upgrading to robust accounting software, focus on finding the right tools and people to support your financial management. You don't need to do it all yourself. Sometimes, the best solution is finding your *who*.

Monitoring Cash Flow

Cash flow, the movement of money in and out of your business, is the lifeblood of any operation. Without adequate cash flow, even profitable businesses can struggle to survive.

Tips for Monitoring and Improving Cash Flow:

- **Invoice Promptly**: Ensure you invoice clients promptly after completing work and follow up on any late payments. Consider setting up a system that allows invoices to be sent with direct payment options built in. For recurring revenue streams, find a way to securely capture customers' credit or debit card information for automatic billing and payment processing.

  For example, in my business, students who make monthly tuition payments are billed through an automated direct draft system. Keep in mind that there are regulations governing the collection and protection of customer payment information. It's essential to implement a system that meets these legal standards to safeguard data and maintain customer trust.

- **Negotiate Payment Terms**: If possible, negotiate terms with suppliers that allow you to pay later, giving you more time to collect payments from your customers.

- **Manage Inventory Wisely**: For businesses that hold inventory, keeping only what you need helps reduce storage costs and frees up cash.

- **Diversify Revenue Streams**: Don't rely solely on one product or service. Diversifying can provide stability and help offset slower periods.

Real-Life Example: Bill, a firefighter/paramedic who also runs a home inspection service, struggled with cash flow issues due to delayed payments. He initially relied on sending physical invoices by mail after completing inspections, which led to long waits for payment and the hassle of chasing down clients. Realizing this inefficiency was holding his business back, I worked with him to implement an online invoicing and payment system that dramatically improved his cash flow.

The Transformation

1. **Immediate Invoicing**: He set up an online system that automatically generated and sent invoices as soon as he completed an inspection. Clients received the invoice immediately, making it easier and faster to process payments.

2. **Conditional Report Delivery**: To further ensure prompt payment, the inspection report was only released to the client once payment was received. This created a clear, professional process that incentivized timely payment without requiring follow-ups.

3. **Credit Card Integration**: He took it a step further by requiring new clients to provide a credit card on file before the inspection. Once the job was complete, the system automatically billed their

card, eliminating the need for manual invoicing altogether. This not only sped up payments but also reduced administrative tasks, allowing him to focus on growing his business.

Results: With these changes, he not only solved his cash flow problems but also streamlined his operations. The switch to online invoicing and credit card payments made it easier for clients to pay and drastically reduced the time he spent managing unpaid bills. It also projected a more professional image for his business, building trust and credibility with his clients.

KEY TAKEAWAY: Efficiency is the cornerstone of a successful business, especially for entrepreneurs juggling multiple roles, like Bill. By removing payment barriers and automating processes, you can solve cash flow issues and free up time to focus on scaling your business. Streamlined systems don't just make your life easier; they make your business more profitable.

Planning for Taxes

Taxes can be complex, especially for new business owners. It's vital to set aside a portion of your earnings for taxes throughout the year. Consulting with an accountant or tax professional can ensure you're in compliance with local, state, and federal tax regulations.

Tax Tips for First Responder Entrepreneurs:

- **Estimated Taxes:** Pay estimated taxes quarterly to avoid a large tax bill at the end of the year. If you don't pay your quarterlies, that is ok. However, if you have a large tax bill at the end of the year, the IRS will fine you for not paying the quarterlies.

As a business owner, you're responsible for paying estimated taxes to the IRS on a quarterly basis. These payments cover your income tax and self-employment tax, including Social Security and Medicare. The IRS expects business owners to pay taxes as income is earned, not just at the end of the year. If you skip quarterly payments and end up with a large tax bill, you may be subject to penalties and interest for underpayment, even if you pay your full tax amount by the filing deadline.

To avoid surprises and fines, calculate your estimated taxes each quarter based on your income, expenses, and anticipated profit. You can use IRS Form 1040-ES or tax software to help you do this. Many accounting programs will also track your earnings and suggest how much to set aside. It's a good idea to set up a separate savings account specifically for taxes and consistently deposit a percentage of your income into it; generally, twenty-five to thirty percent is a safe target. Planning ahead makes tax season far less stressful and helps you maintain healthy cash flow throughout the year.

- **Deductions**: Take advantage of deductions such as home office expenses, business mileage, and equipment costs. How your business is set up in the beginning (e.g., LLC vs. S corp.) can have some real tax advantages. You may have to seek out advice from a tax professional to understand which is best for you.

- **Keep Detailed Records**: Maintain thorough records of all business expenses to make tax preparation easier and maximize deductions.

PRO TIP: Use a dedicated credit card for business expenses to simplify tracking and categorization.

Opt for a card that offers rewards, as these can add significant value over time. For instance, I've accumulated millions of miles on Delta and American Airlines simply by using my business credit card for purchases. Additionally, I leverage a platform like Bill.com, which allows me to pay business bills with my credit card, earning points even on expenses such as our business real estate lease.

You might be surprised at how quickly these points can add up. While there is often a fee associated with using credit cards for payments, the benefits often outweigh the costs. For example, my wife and I are using our accrued miles to fly business class to Tokyo to attend a conference. The rewards you earn can open opportunities for travel or other perks that enrich both your personal and professional life.

Building a Financial Safety Net

Just as you plan for unforeseen challenges in your role as a first responder, having a financial safety net for your business is crucial. An emergency fund can cover unexpected expenses, slow sales periods, or other challenges that could impact your business's cash flow.

How to Build an Emergency Fund:

- **Set a Savings Goal**: Aim to set aside at least three to six months' worth of operating expenses. This can be tough in the startup phase, but is something to strive for.

- **Automate Savings**: Set up automatic transfers to a business savings account to build your safety net over time.

- **Reinvest Wisely**: Once your emergency fund is established, consider reinvesting profits into growth opportunities that align with your long-term goals. We could never have grown into the organization we are today if I had not reinvested our profits in our business.

People Management: Building and Leading Your Team

As your business grows, you'll likely need to expand your team to handle various aspects of operations. Leading people effectively is critical to scaling your business, and your experience as a first responder has already equipped you with strong leadership and teamwork skills that can be invaluable.

Hiring the Right People

Building a strong team begins with hiring the right individuals. Look for candidates who not only have the necessary skills but also align with your business's mission and values. As a first responder, you understand the importance of trust and reliability, so prioritize these qualities in your hiring process.

Interview Tips:

- **Ask Behavioral Questions**: Use questions that reveal how candidates handle challenges, such as, "Can you describe a time when you had to solve a complex problem under pressure?"

- **Assess Cultural Fit**: Look for candidates who will contribute positively to your work environment and share your commitment to quality and service.

Example: In my EMS education business, I discovered that hiring current and retired EMTs and paramedics as instructors not only enhanced our credibility but also fostered a team culture deeply rooted in shared experiences and mutual trust. These individuals bring a wealth of real-world knowledge and authenticity to the classroom, bridging the gap between textbook concepts and practical application. Their firsthand experiences resonate with students, creating a richer and more engaging learning environment.

Moreover, offering roles to retired or injured first responders provides them with a renewed sense of purpose. Many of these professionals, often sidelined by injuries or the natural progression of their careers, still have so much to contribute. Their stories and insights are invaluable in preparing the next generation of EMS providers for the realities of the job. They help students not just learn the skills but also understand the nuances of the role, from managing high-stress situations to providing compassionate care under pressure.

This approach also strengthens our organizational culture and reinforces our mission. When educators have lived the very roles our students are training for, it creates a powerful alignment of purpose. It's not just about teaching, it's about passing on a legacy, instilling pride in the profession, and ensuring that the next wave of EMTs and paramedics enters the field with both the skills and the mindset to excel.

Delegating Responsibility

Once you've built your team, it's essential to trust them to do their jobs. Micromanaging can stifle productivity and lead to frustration. Empower your team by giving them the autonomy to make decisions within their scope of work.

PRO TIP: Use project management tools to assign tasks, track progress, and facilitate communication without micromanaging.

Fostering a Positive Work Environment

A positive work environment can greatly impact your team's morale and productivity. Clear communication, regular feedback, and recognition for hard work can create an atmosphere in which people feel motivated and supported.

Tips for Building a Strong Work Environment:

- **Hold Regular Team Meetings**: Keep everyone on the same page and provide a forum for sharing ideas and addressing concerns.

- **Encourage Open Communication**: Create a space where team members feel comfortable voicing their opinions and suggestions.

- **Celebrate Successes**: Acknowledge both small wins and major milestones to keep morale high.

Training and Development

Just as continuous training is a vital part of your role as a first responder, investing in your team's growth and development is essential for your business. Providing opportunities for training and professional development helps your employees enhance their skills and contribute more effectively.

Ideas for Training Programs:

- **Workshops and Seminars**: Host in-house training sessions or send your team to relevant workshops.

- **Online Courses**: Invest in online courses or webinars that cover skills relevant to your industry.

- **Cross-Training**: Encourage team members to learn different aspects of the business, enhancing collaboration and flexibility.

Managing Conflict

Conflicts can arise in any team, and your ability to manage and resolve them is crucial for maintaining a healthy work environment. Use the same problem-solving skills you apply in the field: stay calm, listen to all perspectives, and work toward a resolution that benefits everyone involved.

> **PRO TIP:** Address conflicts promptly and professionally to foster growth and improve team dynamics.

Conflicts, if left unresolved, can fester and lead to tension, mistrust, and discord within your team. As a leader, it's your responsibility to tackle these issues head-on. While such conversations are seldom easy, addressing conflicts early ensures they don't escalate into larger problems that could undermine morale and productivity.

From my experience, the key to resolving conflicts effectively is preparation and professionalism. Here's how to approach these challenging situations:

1. **Address Issues Early**: Don't delay. The longer you wait, the more entrenched the problem becomes. Early intervention demonstrates your commitment to maintaining a healthy team environment and reinforces accountability.

2. **Prepare Talking Points**: Before the meeting, write down key points in bullet form. This helps you stay focused on the specific issues at hand and ensures you address the core concerns without veering off track.

3. **Stick to Facts**: Keep the conversation rooted in objective observations and concrete examples. Avoid making generalized statements or assumptions about the individual's character or intentions. For example, instead of saying, "You're unreliable," focus on a specific behavior: "I've noticed that deadlines have been missed three times this month. Is everything ok?"

4. **Avoid Personal Attacks**: It's crucial to address the behavior or issue, not the person's personality. Criticism directed at someone's character can cause defensiveness and derail the conversation. Your goal is to encourage improvement, not create further conflict.

5. **Stay Calm and Professional**: Emotions can run high during difficult conversations, but as a leader, you must model composure. Speak calmly, listen actively, and show empathy where appropriate. Remember, your role is to guide the team member toward a resolution, not to win an argument.

6. **Focus on Solutions**: End the conversation by collaboratively identifying actionable steps to address the issue. This approach not only resolves the immediate conflict but also reinforces a culture of accountability and growth.

Effective conflict resolution strengthens your team and enhances trust. By addressing challenges early and approaching them with professionalism and empathy, you transform difficult moments into opportunities for growth, for both the individual and the team as a whole.

Chapter Thoughts

Managing your time, finances, and people is crucial for the success of any business. As a first responder, you already have the skills and mindset needed to handle these responsibilities with discipline and efficiency. By applying the strategies discussed in this chapter, you'll create a solid foundation that allows your business to grow while balancing your personal and professional life.

In the next chapter, we'll take an in-depth look at the financial aspects of entrepreneurship, how to secure funding, manage profitability, and plan for long-term financial success. Your journey as a first responder-entrepreneur is unique and requires a blend of determination, strategy, and adaptability. You've come this far: let's keep building toward your vision.

CHAPTER 8

Navigating Financials—From Funding to Profitability

Financial management is the backbone of every business. While having a great idea and a solid execution plan are essential, the long-term success of your business hinges on sound financial strategies. As a first responder, you're accustomed to working with limited resources and making critical decisions under pressure, skills that translate well into navigating the financial side of entrepreneurship. In this chapter, we'll explore how to secure funding, manage profitability, and develop a long-term financial plan that keeps your business sustainable and thriving.

Understanding Your Startup Costs

Before you can secure funding or turn a profit, you need a clear understanding of your startup costs—the initial expenses required to get your business off the ground. Knowing these upfront costs helps prevent unexpected expenses and lays the groundwork for a sustainable financial strategy. While each business has unique needs, here are some common startup expenses to consider:

1. Equipment and Supplies

Depending on the type of business, you may need to invest in equipment, tools, or specialized supplies. For example, if you're launching a safety consulting firm, you might need presentation materials, training tools, or industry-specific software. For a home services business, equipment could include power tools, vehicles, or cleaning supplies. Make a comprehensive list of everything required to perform your services or produce your products.

2. Legal and Licensing Fees

To operate legally, you'll likely need to register your business and apply for various permits and licenses. Depending on your location and industry, you may face specific regulatory requirements. These costs should be factored into your budget early to avoid legal hurdles later. Consult with a business attorney to understand the legal framework for your industry. In my business, we had both state and national accreditation, both requiring annual fees to be paid to their organizations. As mentioned previously, we are heavily regulated by the OEMS of the Department of Health. In the startup phase of our business, I had to navigate the finer points of state and national accreditation. This was a bear in the beginning, and took hours of diligence to ensure we could be compliant in all facets of our business. There are also state and federal laws that must be followed when hiring people. You have to explore all aspects as they pertain to your business.

3. Marketing and Branding

Building your brand and reaching your target audience often requires an upfront investment in marketing. This may include costs for logo design, website development, social media setup, advertising, and printed materials. Marketing expenses are essential for creating a strong market presence from the outset, so allocate enough funds to establish a professional and memorable brand. Committing financial resources to this area of your business will certainly bring financial reward in the future.

4. Technology and Software

Successful businesses thrive on efficiency, and in today's world, efficiency is often driven by technology. Whether it's accounting software, customer relationship management (CRM) systems, project management tools, or specialized industry software, the right technology can streamline workflows, improve communication, and enhance overall productivity. Investing in reliable, scalable tech solutions early on can save countless hours of manual work, reduce errors, and allow your team to focus on what truly matters: growing the business and serving your customers.

One of the most critical lessons I have learned in business is to choose technology that can scale with you. Switching platforms repeatedly as you grow is costly, time-consuming, and disruptive to operations. That is why we have used **Zoho** as our CRM for over a decade. Zoho is a company with a strong growth mindset, constantly improving its software to meet the evolving needs of businesses. Over the years, we have integrated multiple Zoho products into our operations, allowing us to manage everything from sales tracking to customer support in one unified system.

One of the most impactful tools we have adopted is Calendly, a scheduling platform that allows our students to book appointments directly with our staff. Before using this system, scheduling meetings was an administrative headache. There were countless back-and-forth emails, missed connections, and wasted time trying to coordinate availability. With Calendly, students can now schedule their own appointments based on preset availability, and the system automatically sends reminders to both the student and staff. This small but powerful automation has significantly improved communication and streamlined our student interactions.

When selecting technology for your business, focus on tools that align with your long-term vision. Look for platforms that integrate well with other systems you use, provide excellent customer support, and offer room for expansion. The goal is to create a seamless infrastructure that supports your business today while being robust enough to scale with you in the future. By leveraging the right technology, you can increase efficiency, improve customer experience, and set your business up for sustained success.

5. Working Capital

Working capital is the cash reserve needed to cover day-to-day operating expenses, such as rent, utilities, salaries, and inventory replenishment, while your business ramps up. Ensuring you have enough working capital is critical to sustaining operations during the early stages when revenue may be limited. Estimate how much cash flow you need for at least three to six months to avoid financial strain.

When I started my business, I had only two months' worth of working capital in the bank. It was a risk not to have more, but I believed it was a risk worth taking because I was confident in my ability to generate revenue quickly. Sometimes, you simply must take the leap and start, even if it means stepping into uncertain territory. With careful planning and determination, calculated risks can lead to great rewards.

PRO TIP: Create a detailed startup budget and use it as a baseline to track actual expenses versus projections. This will help you monitor costs, adjust spending as needed, and stay on track financially. (If you create a business plan, this will be in it.)

Securing Funding: Options for First Responders

Not every entrepreneur has the means to self-fund a business, so securing external funding can be essential. The type of funding you choose will depend on your business needs, growth potential, and willingness to take on debt or give up equity. Here are several options available to you:

1. Personal Savings

Using personal savings is often the simplest way to fund a startup, as it eliminates the need for debt or equity dilution. However, if you choose this route, ensure you have enough savings to cover both your business and personal expenses comfortably. Dipping too deep into personal funds without backup savings can lead to financial strain.

Example: I started our business by using personal savings, liquidating assets, and borrowing $10,000 from my parents. This approach allowed me to avoid taking on external debt and retain full control of the business. However, I made sure to stick to a clear budget to avoid overspending on non-essentials. It's easy in the startup phase to feel like you *need* certain things, but often those items can wait. In the early months, it's crucial to prioritize spending on the "must-haves" that directly support your business operations, and hold off on the "nice-to-haves" until your working capital allows for it.

2. Friends and Family

Turning to friends or family for financial support can be effective, but it's essential to approach this option with professionalism. Clearly communicate terms, expectations, and repayment timelines to avoid misunderstandings or strained relationships. Drafting a formal agreement, even among family, helps to establish boundaries and accountability.

3. Business Loans

Traditional business loans from banks or credit unions offer a reliable source of funding, typically at reasonable interest rates. However, they often require strong credit, collateral, and a well-prepared business plan. If you're confident in your revenue projections and ability to repay the loan, this can be a viable option.

Alternative Loan Options:

- **SBA Loans**: Small Business Administration (SBA) loans offer low-interest, government-backed loans specifically designed for small businesses. These loans typically require good credit but offer favorable terms.

  - Be aware: These loans also require you to personally guarantee the repayment, meaning that even if your business fails, you will still have to pay back the loan. You may discharge the loan in bankruptcy, but if you used any collateral (like your personal home), the SBA will put a lien on the property, and that cannot be discharged via bankruptcy. I am not saying this is a bad product, but you should have full transparency when choosing an SBA loan.

- **Microloans**: Organizations like Kiva or local economic development agencies offer microloans, at smaller loan amounts for new and small businesses that may not qualify for traditional bank loans.

4. Grants

Some organizations, especially those focused on small businesses, veterans, or first responders, offer grants that don't need to be repaid. Grants are competitive, but they can provide funding without the burden of debt. Check with local business development centers, government agencies, and private foundations to see if you qualify.

5. Crowdfunding

Crowdfunding platforms like Kickstarter and GoFundMe enable entrepreneurs to raise funds from a large pool of people, often in exchange for early product access or perks. This approach can be especially effective for businesses with strong community support or innovative products. Crowdfunding not only provides funding but also helps build a community of early supporters.

6. Investors

If you're open to giving up a share of your business, investors can provide capital in exchange for equity. Venture capitalists and angel investors are typically interested in high-growth businesses with scalable models. Investors bring not only money but often valuable business expertise and connections.

Investor Considerations:

- **Growth Potential**: Investors are more likely to back businesses with significant expansion potential.

- **Equity Ownership**: Be clear about how much equity you're willing to give up and the level of control you'll retain.

- **Long-Term Vision Alignment**: Look for investors who align with your values and vision to avoid potential conflicts.

Planning for Profitability

After securing funding, the next step is to focus on reaching profitability. Profitability occurs when your revenue exceeds your expenses, generating a surplus that can be reinvested or distributed as income. Let's explore strategies to achieve profitability in your business.

1. Identify Revenue Streams

Think beyond a single revenue source. Identifying multiple streams can diversify your income and reduce financial risk. For example, a safety consulting firm could generate revenue through training workshops, online courses, and one-on-one consulting services. Similarly, a handyman business might offer seasonal packages or add-on services to enhance value for clients. However, having multiple revenue streams doesn't mean running multiple businesses; it's about expanding within your niche. Be mindful not to dilute your focus: adding too many services can distract from your core strengths and potentially limit your highest revenue opportunities.

Example: A first responder who runs a fitness coaching business might generate revenue from in-person classes, online programs, and merchandise sales.

2. Develop a Pricing Strategy

Your pricing strategy plays a significant role in profitability. Price too low, and you'll struggle to cover costs; price too high, and you may lose potential customers. Consider factors like market rates, competitor pricing, production costs, and the unique value you provide to set competitive yet profitable rates.

PRO TIP: Don't be afraid to adjust pricing over time.

If demand exceeds supply or if you're adding new features, a price increase may be justified. I work with an accounting company that every year adds a cost-of-living adjustment to our monthly payment based on the current rate of inflation.

3. Perform a Break-Even Analysis

A break-even analysis calculates the point at which total revenue equals total costs, helping you understand how much you need to sell to cover your expenses. By knowing your break-even point, you can set realistic sales goals and identify how much revenue is needed to achieve profitability. In the early stages of my business, I would project my break-even point based on how many students I needed to sign up. It allowed me to breathe easier when I hit those numbers, many times exceeding the break-even points. When that happens, you are profitable.

4. Control Expenses

Effective cost management is crucial to maintaining profitability. Regularly review your expenses and identify areas where you can cut costs without sacrificing quality. This might include negotiating better supplier terms, automating tasks to reduce labor costs, or eliminating non-essential expenses.

Examples of Cost-Saving Measures:

- **Bulk Purchasing**: Buying materials in bulk can reduce per-unit costs. Just like going to Costco for your household needs, you can do this in your business and buy in larger quantities to reduce the cost per item.

- **Automating Administrative Tasks**: Automating invoicing or payroll can save time and reduce overhead.

- **Outsourcing Selective Functions**: Outsourcing tasks like social media management or accounting can be more affordable than hiring full-time staff. These tasks can be a time suck, so while you may do these yourself in the startup phase, as soon as you are profitable, you should consider turning them over to someone else.

Cash Flow Management

Cash flow refers to the movement of money in and out of your business. It's one of the most critical aspects of financial health. Even if your business is profitable on paper, poor cash flow can lead to unpaid bills, missed payroll, and potential bankruptcy.

1. Maintain a Cash Reserve

Just as you would save for emergencies in your personal life, your business needs a financial buffer. A cash reserve helps you cover unexpected expenses or navigate low cash flow periods. Aim to save enough to cover three to six months of operating expenses. Be mindful of this: as your business grows, so should your cash reserves.

2. Invoice Promptly and Follow Up

For businesses that rely on invoicing, it's crucial to send invoices immediately after work is completed and follow up on overdue payments. Quick invoicing and diligent follow-ups improve cash flow by minimizing the delay between the rendering of services and receipt of payment.

Example: I needed a new landscaper for my home, so late one night, I posted in our town's Facebook group asking for recommendations for a reputable company in the area. At 10:45 p.m., I received a message from Nelson, who said he owned a small business and worked in my neighborhood. What immediately stood out to me was his hustle, grinding at 10:45 p.m. He was my kind of guy! Whether he was desperate for work or fully committed to growing his business, I admired his determination.

We scheduled an appointment, and he came out to provide an estimate. We hit it off right away, and I decided to hire him. When we discussed billing, he explained that the easiest method for him was Venmo. Each week, he would text me after finishing the lawn, and I could send payment that way. While this worked for a few weeks, I quickly realized it wasn't ideal. I travel frequently, and his texts were getting buried in the flood of messages I receive daily. I asked if he could accept credit cards and set up automatic billing, but unfortunately, he didn't have a system like that in place.

Recognizing the opportunity to improve his process, we had a great conversation about it. I asked if he ever struggled with late payments, and unsurprisingly, he said it was a common issue. He was constantly chasing clients for overdue invoices. I suggested he look into an invoicing system that could securely store customer credit card information and automate payments. He took the advice, researched his options, and implemented a system that allowed clients to set up automatic billing.

Now, I no longer have to think about payments. After each service, I simply receive a paid invoice in my email. For him, the change has been transformative. He spends far less time following up on overdue payments, and more time focusing on growing his business. It's a win–win for both of us, and a perfect example of how the right systems can streamline operations and improve customer satisfaction.

PRO TIP: Don't make it difficult for customers to pay you.

I didn't want to Venmo my landscaper every week, especially since I travel frequently. I knew his texts reminding me to pay could easily get lost in the flood of messages I receive daily. Consider your own business: what systems can you implement to make it as easy as possible for customers to pay? The fewer barriers they encounter, the faster and more consistently you'll get paid. Simplifying payment processes isn't just convenient for your clients; it's good for your cash flow, too.

3. Monitor Accounts Payable

While prompt payment from clients is vital, strategically managing when you pay your own bills is equally important. In the startup phase of my business, when managing working capital was critical, I took full advantage of favorable payment terms from suppliers, such as net thirty or net sixty days. I avoided paying bills earlier than necessary unless it offered a discount. This approach helped conserve cash flow during those crucial early months.

Now that our cash flow is strong, we've adjusted our strategy. In most cases, we pay bills as they come in, unless a specific receivable is tied to that expense and is outstanding. For example, if we're waiting on payment from a client that covers a particular expense, we'll align the payment timing accordingly. However, for most of our bills, especially those from small businesses we work with, I ensure they're paid promptly. I understand they depend on timely payments just as much as we do, and it's a way to support the ecosystem of small businesses that keep everything running smoothly.

4. Forecast Cash Flow

Regularly reviewing and forecasting cash flow is essential for anticipating financial challenges and opportunities. A cash flow forecast provides an estimate of your future income and expenses, allowing you to plan for upcoming financial needs, allocate resources strategically, and identify the right moments for investment. While it may not be an exact science, it serves as a crucial tool in assessing your current financial situation, analyzing past revenue trends, and incorporating projected growth to create a realistic financial roadmap.

During the rapid growth phases of my business, forecasting cash flow often felt more like an educated guess than a precise calculation. We were scaling quickly and money was coming in fast, but it was also going out just as quickly. Expansion required significant reinvestment, whether in staffing, infrastructure, or new technology. Even as revenue soared, so did our expenses, making cash flow management more critical than ever.

One of the most challenging aspects of forecasting during growth is ensuring that profitability remains in balance. There were times when our expenses outpaced our revenue, creating a temporary squeeze on cash flow. However, by closely monitoring enrollment trends, program waitlists, and upcoming revenue streams, I could confidently project that this shortfall was temporary. I knew that within a couple of months, our next round of programs would be fully booked, and the financial picture would stabilize.

KEY TAKEAWAY: Cash flow forecasting is not just about crunching numbers, it's about understanding the patterns of your business, recognizing cycles of investment and return, and making informed decisions that support sustainable growth. By consistently reviewing cash flow, adjusting for market changes, and staying ahead of financial needs, you can ensure your business remains agile and well-positioned for long-term success.

Preparing for Growth

Once your business achieves profitability and has consistent cash flow, it's time to think about growth. Whether expanding your product line, reaching new markets, or hiring more staff, growth requires a solid financial foundation and careful planning.

Instead of viewing all profits as income, consider reinvesting a portion back into your business. Reinvestment is one of the most effective ways to support sustainable growth. It can fund new equipment, expand your marketing efforts, facilitate hiring, or enhance operational systems. Personally, I take a reasonable salary from the business, as required by the IRS for an S corporation. Beyond that, I've made it a priority to reinvest retained earnings into the business year after year.

Many business owners see their "profit" at the end of the year and are tempted to pull it all out as a distribution. While enjoying the fruits of your labor is important, having a growth mindset and a long-term perspective is vital to the future of your business. From the day we opened, I understood that the only way to scale and improve was to consistently reinvest, whether in equipment, systems, or people.

If you were to visit our business today, you'd see the tangible results of that reinvestment. Every piece of equipment, every resource, every innovative system we have in place was purchased with retained earnings. What's more, we bought it all with cash. This deliberate choice to operate debt-free has given us a significant advantage, offering both financial stability and the freedom to make decisions without the constraints or pressures of servicing debt, meaning paying a monthly loan payment.

A Case for Debt: Strategic Leverage in Real Estate

That said, I'm not entirely opposed to debt. In our short-term rental business, I've strategically used debt (or **leverage**) to finance the purchase of real estate. The key difference here lies in the type of business and the cash flow it generates. For our rental property, I project cash flow from the business to cover the debt payments. This approach ensures that the property effectively pays for itself while still generating income.

There are also significant tax advantages to using debt in a real estate business, including the ability to deduct depreciation and interest expenses. These benefits must be considered carefully when making such investments. While operating debt-free works for my education business, leveraging debt in the short-term rental space has been a powerful tool for growth in a different context.

Finding the Balance

Ultimately, the decision to reinvest profits or use debt depends on your business model, goals, and financial strategy. Reinvesting retained earnings can provide financial independence, ensuring your business grows year after year without external financing. On the other hand, leveraging debt in the right context, like a rental property with reliable cash flow, can unlock opportunities that might otherwise be out of reach.

KEY TAKEAWAY: Align your financial strategies with your long-term vision. Whether you choose reinvestment, strategic debt, or a combination of the two, staying focused on sustainable growth will position your business for long-term success.

Why Capital Investments Matter

Capital investments are critical for scaling your business and staying competitive. For example:

- Upgrading equipment can improve efficiency and output.

- Expanding office space may allow you to accommodate a growing team or serve more clients.

- Investing in technology can streamline operations, reduce costs, and enhance the customer experience.

Without planning, these necessary upgrades can create financial stress, disrupt cash flow, or lead to rushed decisions that don't align with your long-term goals.

| How to Plan for Capital Investments

The following are some actionable strategies to plan for and execute capital investments effectively:

1. Forecast Future Needs

Evaluate your business's growth trajectory and anticipate future needs. For example:

- If you're hiring more staff, consider how much space you'll need and when.

- If demand for your product or service is increasing, assess whether your current equipment can keep up or if upgrades are necessary.

- Identify bottlenecks in your current operations that could be resolved with additional assets.

In my business, our growth created a significant space problem for the business, both for our personnel and our students. We simply outgrew our existing facilities. It became clear that we needed more room, but we had to be intentional about envisioning what our future would look like based on our past growth trajectory. As we began exploring larger real estate options, we focused on anticipating our space needs for the next ten years. This forward-looking approach proved invaluable when negotiating with building owners, who were seeking tenants willing to commit to a ten-year lease. A long-term lease gave us leverage to negotiate favorable terms, including allowances for the buildout of the new space.

We were eyeing a development of over 18,000 square feet for our school. This wasn't our first encounter with this particular building; three years earlier, during a period of explosive growth from 2018 to 2020, we had leased approximately 6,000 square feet in the same building on a short-term three-year lease. At the time, it served as overflow space to accommodate our expansion, supplementing our primary location, which had 7,500 square feet. To align our strategy, I ensured that both leases, the 6,000 square feet in the overflow building and our primary space, expired at the same time, allowing us to consolidate operations under one roof if necessary.

When we began evaluating our ten-year plan, the existing 6,000 square feet in the building factored heavily into the decision. My COO, Lindsay, and I made detailed projections about the business's future needs. While we were confident in our growth trajectory, we couldn't predict with certainty whether we'd need to retain the additional 6,000 square feet, giving us a potential total of 24,000 square feet in the building. As negotiations progressed, I analyzed our company's finances in detail to determine whether we could afford both the 18,000-square-foot first-floor space and the additional 6,000 square feet on the second floor. The answer was a resounding yes, and knowing this gave us additional leverage in our discussions with the building owners.

In the end, we reached an excellent deal. We secured a ten-year lease for the 18,000 square feet on the first floor and extended the lease on the 6,000 square feet on the second floor for an additional two years. The building owners were eager to retain us as tenants, and the long-term commitment worked in their favor as well. They offered us highly favorable terms on both spaces, including generous financial allowances for the tenant buildout of the first-floor space.

This negotiation was a win for both parties. The owners retained us in the building for another two years in the second-floor space while securing a long-term tenant for the 18,000-square-foot first-floor space. For us, it provided the room we needed to support our continued growth while allowing us to create a beautiful, functional space for our students and staff.

In hindsight, retaining the second-floor space was the right move. Our growth has continued, and we've realized that having the additional 6,000 square feet is vital. As we approach the expiration of that lease, we fully intend to renew it, ensuring we have the capacity to meet the needs of our expanding operations.

2. Create a Capital Budget

A capital budget outlines your expected expenditures on large assets and helps prioritize which investments to make and when. Include:

- estimated costs of the assets you plan to purchase

- potential financing options, such as retained earnings, loans, or leasing

- projected ROI (return on investment) to evaluate the value each investment will bring to your business

Example: A growing landscaping business might create a capital budget to replace aging mowers and purchase a larger trailer to accommodate increased work volume. The ROI is calculated based on the time, maintenance, and labor saved by using newer, more efficient equipment.

3. Build a Reserve Fund

Set aside a portion of your profits each month for future capital investments. A reserve fund allows you to make purchases without depleting working capital or relying entirely on loans.

Example: A small gym owner saves ten percent of monthly profits into a reserve fund earmarked for upgrading exercise equipment. Over time, this fund grows, enabling them to make purchases without taking on debt.

4. Explore Financing Options

Sometimes, paying outright for a large investment isn't feasible or the best financial strategy. Explore financing options that suit your business's needs, such as:

- **Loans**: A small business loan can help fund major purchases while allowing you to spread costs over time.

- **Leasing**: Leasing equipment or vehicles may be a better option if the asset will require frequent upgrades.

- **Equipment Financing**: Some vendors offer financing specifically for their products, often with competitive rates.

Example: A video production company might lease high-end cameras instead of purchasing them outright, ensuring they have access to the latest technology without a large upfront cost.

5. Plan for Depreciation

Capital investments often come with tax advantages through depreciation, which allows you to deduct a portion of the asset's cost over its useful life. Work with an accountant to ensure you're leveraging these benefits effectively.

Maximizing Tax Benefits with Section 179

For business owners, understanding tax incentives like Section 179 of the IRS tax code can significantly impact financial planning and cash flow management. This provision allows businesses to deduct the full cost of qualifying equipment or machinery in the year it's purchased rather than depreciating it over several years. By leveraging this deduction, you can reduce taxable income, lower your overall tax liability, and free up cash flow. Money that would otherwise have gone to taxes can instead be reinvested into growing your business.

Let's break it down with a real-world example. Suppose you purchase a $100,000 piece of equipment for your business. Under Section 179, you can deduct the full cost of that equipment in the same tax year. Here's how that impacts your financials:

- Your accountant will apply the $100,000 deduction directly to your profit and loss (P&L) statement, reducing your taxable profit by that amount.

- If you operate as an LLC or an S corporation, that deduction will flow through to your personal taxes via your K-1 statement.

- Now, let's assume your business ended the year with a $50,000 profit after all expenses. In an LLC or S corp, that profit passes through to your personal tax return, meaning you'll owe taxes on it, regardless of whether you withdraw the money from the business or retain it as working capital.

- However, thanks to the $100,000 Section 179 deduction, your reported taxable income is now significantly lower. If your personal tax rate is 32 percent, that deduction translates into an actual cash savings of $32,000—money that stays in your pocket rather than going to the IRS.

The Power of Strategic Tax Planning

This is why working with a knowledgeable tax professional is crucial. They can help you plan major purchases strategically, ensuring you time deductions in a way that maximizes savings while maintaining financial stability for your business.

KEY TAKEAWAY: Understanding and applying Section 179 can be a powerful tool in reducing tax burdens, improving cash flow, and reinvesting in your company's future success. Instead of viewing equipment purchases as pure expenses, think of them as financially strategic moves that can help both your business operations and your bottom line.

6. Prioritize Investments with High ROI

Not all capital investments are created equal. Focus on those that provide the most significant return for your business. High-ROI investments typically:

- Increase efficiency or productivity
- Reduce operational costs
- Open new revenue streams

Example: A restaurant owner invests in a point-of-sale (POS) system that integrates inventory management, reducing waste and saving staff time. The ROI comes from lower inventory costs and increased operational efficiency.

7. Phase Investments Gradually

If multiple capital investments are needed, phase them in gradually to avoid overwhelming your resources. Prioritize based on urgency, ROI, and available funding.

Example: A digital marketing agency needing new office space, additional computers, and upgraded software phases its investments over a year. They first purchase computers to support new hires, then upgrade software six months later, and finally move to a larger office once revenue stabilizes.

8. Monitor Cash Flow Before and After

Capital investments often require significant upfront spending, which can impact cash flow. Before making a purchase, review your cash flow to ensure you can manage the expense. Afterward, track how the investment impacts your business to confirm it's delivering the expected benefits.

Example: A home services business invests in a second work van to handle increasing demand. They carefully monitor cash flow before purchasing and then track how the additional vehicle affects their ability to take on more clients and increase revenue.

9. Evaluate Vendor Options

For large purchases, research vendors to find the best deals and service terms. Request multiple quotes and consider factors like warranty, customer support, and long-term reliability, as well as past experiences with a vendor. I personally would rather spend a little more money when I have built a relationship with a vendor and know they will be there to service us if and when we need them. Business is about relationships, and building those relationships creates trust and loyalty.

10. Communicate with Your Team

Clear communication is key if an investment directly impacts your team, whether it's upgrading equipment, implementing new technology, or moving to a larger office. Your team should understand not only the benefits but also the timeline, potential disruptions, and how the change will improve their work environment. Keeping them informed and engaged ensures they feel included in the process rather than blindsided by decisions that affect their day-to-day operations.

I learned this lesson firsthand when we were in the middle of building out a new leased space for our company. At the leadership level, we were deep in planning, discussing office layouts, logistics, and how the expansion would support our growing team. But in all the excitement, I failed to keep the entire staff in the loop.

One day, while casually discussing the progress in the office, I mentioned where everyone's new workspace would be. One of my team members spoke up and said, "I can't wait to see it!" That's when it hit me: not everyone had seen the space yet. Only the leadership team, the key stakeholders in the project, had been involved. The rest of the team, the people who would actually be working in the new space, were completely in the dark.

I immediately course-corrected. I told the team, "Let's take a field trip." We all piled into cars and drove to the new building, where construction crews were still hard at work. As we walked through the space, I explained the vision, where each department would be located, and how the new setup would make their work more efficient and enjoyable. Seeing their reactions—the excitement, the anticipation, the validation that this move was for them—provided a reminder of how powerful transparency and inclusion can be.

I also took a moment to apologize. "We should have done this sooner," I told them. By bringing them into the process earlier, they could have felt more connected to the change, rather than having it presented as a decision made without them. It was a valuable lesson in leadership. When people feel involved, they're more likely to be engaged, excited, and committed to making the transition successful.

As a leader, never underestimate the power of inclusion. The more you bring your team along in the journey, the more invested they'll be in the success of the company. People support what they help create.

Benefits of Planning Capital Investments

When planned strategically, capital investments can:

- **Support Business Growth**: Provide the tools and infrastructure needed to scale operations.

- **Increase Efficiency**: Reduce costs or improve productivity through better equipment or systems.

- **Enhance Customer Experience**: Upgrade services or facilities to meet or exceed client expectations.

- **Strengthen Financial Stability**: Avoid unnecessary debt by aligning purchases with revenue growth and available capital.

Chapter Thoughts

Planning for capital investments is about more than just purchasing assets, it's about aligning your financial strategy with your growth goals. By forecasting needs, creating a budget, building reserves, and prioritizing high-ROI opportunities, you can make confident decisions that drive your business forward. Whether it's upgrading equipment, expanding your workspace, or adopting new technology, thoughtful planning ensures that each investment strengthens your foundation for sustainable success.

Remember, capital investments are not just expenditures; they are investments in the future of your business. With a clear plan in place, you'll be prepared to seize opportunities, overcome challenges, and continue scaling your business with confidence.

In the next chapter, we'll explore overcoming challenges and building resilience—essential skills to help you handle setbacks and continue progressing on your entrepreneurial journey.

CHAPTER 9

Overcoming Challenges–Resilience in Entrepreneurship

Entrepreneurship is a journey filled with highs and lows, triumphs and setbacks. For first responders transitioning into the business world, this path can feel both exciting and daunting. The good news is that the resilience, adaptability, and problem-solving skills you've honed in your career are precisely the tools needed to succeed as an entrepreneur.

This chapter will guide you through handling setbacks, building resilience, and transforming challenges into opportunities. With the right mindset, strategies, and support, you can navigate even the toughest obstacles and emerge stronger. Remember: resiliency is only built by going through hard things. It's like the adage about good judgment and experience: Good judgment comes from experience. Experience comes from bad judgment.

Understanding the Entrepreneurial Landscape

Entrepreneurship is often romanticized as a pursuit of passion and freedom. While these aspects are true, the reality also includes uncertainty, risk, and constant adaptation. Understanding the broader landscape can help you prepare mentally and emotionally for the road ahead.

The Three Realities of Entrepreneurship

1. Uncertainty and Risk

Starting and running a business involves inherent risks. Market conditions can change, unexpected competitors may emerge, and new challenges can arise from external factors, such as economic downturns, COVID-19, or supply chain disruptions. Success depends on your ability to navigate this uncertainty with confidence and adaptability.

2. Emotional Rollercoaster

The entrepreneurial journey is a rollercoaster of emotions, filled with exhilarating highs and challenging lows. Securing a major client or reaching a significant milestone can feel incredibly rewarding, but setbacks like losing a contract or encountering financial difficulties can test your resolve. Maintaining emotional balance isn't just important for your well-being, it's essential for the long-term success of your business. As the leader of your organization, your team will look to you for steadiness, particularly during tough times. Your ability to remain calm and composed will inspire confidence and guide your team through uncertainty.

In my career as a paramedic and fire officer, I learned early on the importance of staying calm in the face of chaos. Whether it was managing a multi-vehicle accident or directing a team in a burning building, my role demanded clarity and composure. The stakes were sometimes life and death, and the people I was tasked to lead, my crew, relied on me to make decisive, level-headed decisions. They needed to trust that I could navigate any situation and provide the leadership required to solve the problem at hand, whether it was a patient in distress or a victim needing rescue.

The same principles apply to entrepreneurship. When challenges arise, your team will look to you for guidance. If you panic or let emotions dictate your actions, it can erode their confidence and magnify the stress of the situation. However, if you model calm, focused leadership, your team will be better equipped to rally together, stay solution-oriented, and overcome obstacles.

Entrepreneurship, like emergency response, requires developing an emotional resilience that allows you to handle setbacks without becoming paralyzed by them. Acknowledge your emotions, but don't let them control you. Instead, channel that energy into constructive action. Remember, your team will follow your lead, so your ability to remain steady in turbulent times can make all the difference in navigating the challenges of running a business.

3. Continuous Learning

Business environments are constantly evolving. Advancements in technology, shifts in consumer behavior, and emerging industry trends mean that yesterday's strategies may no longer be effective tomorrow. To thrive as an entrepreneur, you must commit to ongoing learning, adapting to change, and staying ahead of the curve. This agility isn't just beneficial, it's essential for long-term success.

Think of it like the world of EMS—the fire service, or police department. In these professions, continual education and training are fundamental to staying prepared for new challenges. Whether it's mastering the latest life-saving technique or learning to use cutting-edge equipment, first responders understand the importance of evolving with the demands of their field. Similarly, entrepreneurs must proactively seek out knowledge, embrace innovation, and refine their strategies to remain competitive.

Adapting to a dynamic business landscape requires both curiosity and discipline. Stay informed about industry trends, invest in professional development, and surround yourself with people who challenge you to grow. Just as a firefighter, police officer, or EMT/paramedic wouldn't face an emergency without the right tools and training, an entrepreneur shouldn't approach their business without staying equipped with up-to-date knowledge and a willingness to evolve. In both arenas, the commitment to learning and improvement is what separates success from stagnation.

Building Resilience: Lessons from the Front Lines

Resilience is a hallmark of first responders. Whether responding to a medical emergency, extinguishing a fire, or managing a critical law enforcement situation, you've experienced the intensity of life-and-death moments that demand unwavering focus, quick thinking, and adaptability. These same qualities, honed in high-pressure environments, provide an exceptional foundation for navigating the complexities of entrepreneurship. Let's examine how these traits translate to entrepreneurship.

Calm Under Pressure

In emergency situations, panic isn't an option. As a first responder, you have had to make high-level cognitive decisions in extreme situations, when time was of the essence, all while others were looking to you for leadership.

This ability to remain composed and focused in high-stress scenarios is invaluable when managing a business crisis.

Entrepreneurial Application

In business, crises often arise: a dissatisfied client, a sudden financial shortfall, or a major supplier failing to deliver. The stakes may not be life or death, but your ability to remain composed can be the difference between escalating a problem and solving it efficiently. Calmness allows you to think clearly, weigh options, and make informed decisions.

Real-Life Scenario

Consider a small business owner who suddenly lost a major client representing thirty percent of their revenue. Instead of panicking, they methodically evaluated their expenses, adjusted their budget, and launched a targeted marketing campaign to attract new clients. Within months, they replaced the lost revenue and diversified their income streams to avoid similar risks in the future.

Problem-Solving Skills

On the job, you're trained to quickly identify problems, evaluate options, and implement solutions. In business, these same skills help you tackle operational challenges, customer issues, or strategic decisions.

- **Example**: Suppose a key supplier fails to deliver materials essential to your product. A resilient entrepreneur doesn't dwell on the setback but instead quickly identifies alternative suppliers, negotiates new terms, and ensures minimal disruption to their operations.

One area I encourage you to approach with caution is decision-making in business. As a first responder, you're trained to solve problems in the moment, often with limited information, under intense time pressure, and in situations where lives are at stake. This demand for rapid action is a core part of our profession, but it doesn't always translate directly to the business world.

In business, most decisions aren't as time-sensitive as those you're used to making in the field. As a first responder, you're trained to make rapid choices under pressure, when seconds count, lives are on the line, and delay simply isn't an option. But in the entrepreneurial world, urgency doesn't always equal importance. This is one of the most critical mindset shifts you'll have to make when stepping into business leadership.

Unlike an emergency call, where you may have minutes or seconds to act, business often grants you what's known as **discretionary time**. That means you have the space to slow down, assess the problem thoroughly, seek input, weigh alternatives, and involve your team in the decision-making process. It's not just allowed—it's smart. Slowing down doesn't show weakness, it shows maturity and control. But recognizing when to pause and when to move takes practice.

This is where the **Eisenhower Matrix** we discussed in Chapter 7 becomes a powerful tool. It divides your work into four categories:

1. **Urgent and Important** – Do it now. These are true emergencies, both in the field and in business, like a payroll issue that threatens to delay employee paychecks or a key client at risk of walking away.

2. **Important but Not Urgent** – Plan it. These are strategic, thoughtful decisions, like designing your marketing plan or preparing for a new product launch. These often get pushed aside in the rush of daily operations, but they're where long-term growth lives.

3. **Urgent but Not Important** – Delegate it. These are distractions that feel pressing, like constant emails or routine requests, but don't move your business forward. As your business grows, these are perfect for outsourcing or assigning to your team.

4. **Not Urgent and Not Important** – Eliminate it. These are the tasks that drain time and energy without meaningful return, social media scrolling, or obsessing over things outside your control.

Understanding where your tasks fall within this matrix can be a game-changer. As first responders, almost everything feels like quadrant one, urgent and important. But in business, living in that zone 24/7 leads to burnout and poor decision-making. The real power lies in investing your time in quadrant two: important but not urgent. That's where strategy, vision, and leadership take root.

Learning to discern what truly needs your immediate attention and what can be scheduled, delegated, or even dropped is the mark of a mature business owner. It's how you shift from first responder to architect, building something lasting rather than just putting out daily fires.

This new pace might feel unnatural at first, but embracing it allows you to operate with clarity, purpose, and precision, just like you've done on the street. You already have the instincts. Now you're just applying them in a new environment.

If you take away just one phrase from this book, make it: **There are no HR emergencies**! When faced with personnel issues, do not make any quick or emotional decisions. Take the time you need to get counsel before you get yourself or your organization in trouble.

Adaptability

In the field, plans rarely go as expected. A fire spreads unpredictably, a patient's condition deteriorates, or unforeseen complications arise. Your ability to adapt on the fly is a cornerstone of effective emergency response and a vital skill for entrepreneurship.

Case in Point

During the COVID-19 pandemic, countless businesses had to pivot overnight. Restaurants introduced delivery services, fitness studios launched virtual classes, and retailers shifted to e-commerce. The businesses that adapted quickly not only survived but often thrived in the new landscape.

Application for Entrepreneurs

Adapting doesn't just mean reacting to external changes. It involves anticipating shifts in the market, embracing new technologies, and staying flexible in your business model. For example, a first responder-turned-consultant might explore virtual training platforms to reach a broader audience beyond their local community.

Leading Teams Effectively

As a first responder, you've led teams in high-stakes environments where trust, clear communication, and collaboration are non-negotiable. These leadership qualities are equally essential in business.

Building a Strong Team Culture

Leadership in business goes beyond delegating tasks. It's about creating a culture of trust and shared purpose. Your team should feel supported, valued, and aligned with your business's mission.

When I started my business, I realized that fostering a team culture grounded in shared experiences was critical. By hiring current and retired first responders, we built a team that not only understood the industry but also shared a passion for education. This culture of trust and camaraderie became a cornerstone of our success.

Navigating Common Challenges

While your first responder background equips you with unique strengths, transitioning to entrepreneurship presents its own set of challenges:

- **Time Management:** Balancing your full-time career with building a business can be overwhelming. Prioritize tasks, use time-blocking tools, and delegate where possible.

- **Financial Pressures:** Managing cash flow, securing funding, and ensuring profitability require careful planning and monitoring.

- **Isolation:** Entrepreneurship can be lonely, especially when juggling dual roles. Build a strong support network of peers, mentors, and advisers.

- **Fear of Failure:** The fear of making mistakes can paralyze progress. Embrace failure as a learning opportunity and focus on continuous improvement.

Strategies for Overcoming Setbacks

Challenges are inevitable, but they don't have to define your journey. The following are some proven strategies to navigate and overcome obstacles:

1. Embrace a Growth Mindset

A growth mindset—the belief that challenges are opportunities to learn and grow—is crucial in entrepreneurship.

- **View Challenges as Learning Opportunities**: Every setback provides a lesson. Embrace mistakes as a chance to refine your strategies.

- **Stay Curious**: Continuously seek new knowledge, whether through books, courses, or mentorship. You've got more information at your fingertips than at any previous time in history. Use the internet to learn. Research what other businesses similar to yours are doing. Look at their marketing and product offerings, and see how you can make your business stand out. Use AI to help you curate ideas and research what others are doing in your space.

2. Build a Strong Support Network

You don't have to face challenges alone. Surround yourself with people who can offer advice, encouragement, and practical help.

- **Mentorship**: Connect with experienced entrepreneurs who can provide guidance.

- **Peer Groups**: Join business associations or networking groups to share experiences and learn from others. For me, this was joining a mastermind with other entrepreneurs who helped me navigate through a number of problems in our business.

- **Family and Friends**: Keep your loved ones informed and involved. They can be a vital source of strength for you. Remember that they love you and they want the best for you. On another note, they may also not understand you or what is driving you on a daily basis. Some may offer advice to slow down, take it easy and (my favorite), "Why can't you relax?" They will not understand, as they are not you and probably not entrepreneurs.

3. Hire a Business Coach: Accelerate Your Growth

Engaging a business coach can be one of the most impactful decisions you make as an entrepreneur. A coach provides guidance, accountability, and a fresh perspective, helping you navigate challenges and uncover opportunities that may not be immediately visible.

Why Hire a Business Coach?

- **Accelerated Learning:** A coach can share insights from their own experience, helping you bypass common mistakes and focus on strategies that drive results.

- **Personal and Professional Growth:** Coaches challenge you to step out of your comfort zone, fostering growth in areas that directly impact your business and leadership skills.

- **Objective Perspective:** Sometimes, being immersed in your business makes it difficult to see the bigger picture. A coach offers an external, unbiased perspective, helping you identify blind spots and refine your strategies.

- **Accountability:** A coach ensures you stay focused on your goals and holds you accountable for the decisions and actions needed to achieve success.

My Experience with Business Coaches

Over the past fifteen years, I've worked with several business coaches, each bringing unique insights and value to the table. Every coach I've hired forced me to think differently, pushed me to grow both personally and professionally, and played a pivotal role in taking our business to the next level.

- **New Perspectives:** One coach encouraged me to reevaluate our mission and focus not just on our students but also on the impact they would have on their future patients. This shifted how we communicated our purpose and created a deeper connection to the *why* behind our work.

- **Challenging the Status Quo:** Another coach identified inefficiencies in our processes, prompting us to implement systems that saved time and resources while scaling our operations.

- **Building Confidence:** When I felt stuck or uncertain about major decisions, my coaches provided clarity and encouragement, empowering me to take calculated risks that ultimately paid off.

Choosing the Right Coach

- **Look for Alignment:** Choose a coach whose values and experience align with your business and personal goals.

- **Evaluate Expertise:** Seek someone with a proven track record in your industry or with the specific challenges you're facing.

- **Check Testimonials:** Research feedback from other entrepreneurs who have worked with the coach to ensure they deliver measurable results.

Hiring a business coach is an investment in yourself and your business. The right coach doesn't just help you grow your bottom line; they help you grow as a leader, paving the way for long-term success.

4. Develop Resilience Through Stress Management

Managing stress is critical for maintaining mental and physical health.

- **Exercise Regularly**: Physical activity reduces stress and improves focus.

- **Practice Mindfulness**: Techniques like meditation can help you stay present and balanced. Some of my best ideas have come after a meditation session. It helped clear my mind of the clutter. I use a meditation app, which really helps me focus.

- **Engage in Hobbies**: Taking time for leisure activities can recharge your energy and creativity. This is the hardest thing for me personally. I love to play golf, but I would feel guilty spending five hours on the golf course playing eighteen holes, so I compromise and play nine holes and get back to working on the business when I'm done. I make that time to enjoy the hobby I love so much and feel reenergized to continue to grind when I need to.

5. Learn from Failures

Failure isn't the end; it's a stepping stone to success. Every time we failed at something, we have used it as the basis for a lesson.

Analyze Setbacks: Take the time to thoroughly understand what went wrong and why. In the fire service, we conduct Post-Incident Analysis to review operations, while in EMS, Morbidity and Mortality (M&M) rounds provide a platform to dissect challenging cases, and the police formulate after-action reports. The three processes share a common purpose: identifying what worked, what didn't, and how decisions impacted outcomes.

The approach is structured and reflective. First, we evaluate the issues we encountered—what challenges arose, and how we responded given the information available at the time? Next, we assess the decisions made and their ripple effects, asking key questions: "Did our choices move us closer to resolving the problem?" "Were there missed opportunities or alternative strategies we could have employed?"

By analyzing setbacks with this level of rigor, entrepreneurs can adopt a similar mindset. Treat challenges as opportunities to learn and improve. Look at what information you had when you made decisions, evaluate the effectiveness of those decisions, and consider how you can apply those lessons to future situations. This method not only enhances problem-solving but also fosters a culture of continuous improvement, much like the learning ethos embedded in emergency services.

I've always viewed failures as opportunities to learn and grow. One such lesson came when I challenged my team to create a high-quality video paramedic program for our students. It seemed like an innovative way to improve our educational offerings, but the journey to that goal didn't unfold as I had envisioned.

The idea was sparked after I responded to a fire alarm at a local photography and video business. It turned out to be a false alarm, and as I reset the system, I struck up a conversation with the owner about his business and mine. When I shared my vision for video production and content creation, he assured me it wasn't that hard to achieve and even offered to help set up a recording studio at our school.

His confidence was infectious. He provided a proposal for equipment and installation, and I moved forward, investing tens of thousands of dollars to build the studio. Once it was completed, he gave us a quick tutorial on the equipment and outlined what he claimed was an "easy" process to create professional-grade videos. I thought we were on our way.

The reality, however, was far from the fairytale he described. After months of trying and failing to produce quality videos, I found myself standing in the doorway of our studio, watching my COO and Director of Education painstakingly edit a video. I could see their frustration as they wrestled with unfamiliar tools and processes. It was in that moment that I realized this approach was unsustainable. Something had to change.

Around this time, I had read Dan Sullivan's book, *Who Not How*, and its message hit me like a lightning bolt. As noted earlier, the book's core idea is simple yet powerful: instead of asking, "How can I do this?" you should ask, "Who can help me achieve this?" It was clear we needed someone with expertise in video production to bring our vision to life.

Taking this insight to heart, I posted a job listing for a videographer on Indeed. The response was overwhelming. Hundreds of applications poured in, and I had to shut off the ad within days. Within two weeks, we found the right person to join our team.

Our new video production manager brought immediate value, starting with a comprehensive evaluation of the studio and equipment. Unfortunately, the news wasn't good. Much of the equipment we had purchased, despite being expensive, was not suited to deliver the level of quality we needed. The lighting packages were also inadequate. In short, we had not only failed at making the videos, but also wasted tens of thousands of dollars on the wrong tools.

As painful as this realization was, it became a turning point. This failure forced us to reframe our approach. By focusing on *who* could help rather than struggling with the *how*, we pivoted toward a more sustainable and professional strategy. Our new hire reconfigured the studio, sourced the right equipment, and established a streamlined workflow that aligned with our vision.

In hindsight, this experience taught me that failure isn't the end—it's a lesson. We may have started off on the wrong foot, but the adjustments we made turned that setback into an opportunity for growth. It's a reminder that investing in the right people is often the key to unlocking your vision and achieving your goals.

Set Realistic Goals

Unrealistic expectations can lead to frustration and burnout. Break your vision into manageable steps.

- **Short-Term Goals**: Focus on achievable milestones that build momentum.

- **Long-Term Goals**: Keep your eyes on the bigger picture, even when progress feels slow.

Turning challenges into opportunities is a hallmark of entrepreneurial resilience. Every obstacle you face has the potential to spark growth, inspire innovation, and refine your business practices. Setbacks often push you to think creatively, leading to solutions or strategies you might not have considered otherwise. For instance, a safety consultant experiencing declining attendance at workshops could pivot to developing online training programs, thereby reaching a broader audience and opening new revenue streams.

Similarly, difficulties can hone your skills and build confidence. A marketing misstep, for example, might highlight the importance of understanding your target audience, ultimately leading to more effective marketing campaigns in the future. Successfully navigating these hurdles not only strengthens your capabilities but also enhances your credibility, demonstrating resilience and reliability to customers and peers alike.

Resilience is a skill that can be cultivated with intentional effort, but it's also forged in adversity. As a first responder, you know firsthand that true resilience isn't theoretical; it's built through lived experience, often in the face of chaos, stress, and uncertainty. But just as your training prepares you to respond under pressure, you can also train yourself to be resilient in business. Start by developing emotional intelligence, which involves understanding and managing your own emotions while empathizing with others.

Self-awareness helps you recognize your triggers and reactions, while empathy strengthens your ability to lead and connect with your team. Financial preparedness also plays a vital role. Maintaining a safety net of three to six months of business expenses can ease anxiety during slow seasons or unexpected challenges. Together, these practices create a durable foundation, one that enables you not just to endure difficult moments, but to emerge stronger, wiser, and more capable each time you face them.

Case Study: Sarah's Safety Consulting Firm

Sarah, a paramedic with over a decade of field experience, saw a growing demand for workplace safety training. Inspired by her first responder background, she envisioned a business that provided comprehensive safety training to small and medium-sized businesses. However, she faced significant challenges, particularly in balancing her demanding paramedic shifts with the needs of her growing business.

The Challenge

Initially, Sarah tried to do everything herself: deliver training, create marketing materials, manage her website, and handle administrative tasks like scheduling and invoicing. This led to long days, frequent exhaustion, and a constant feeling of being overwhelmed. As her client base expanded, the workload became unsustainable, and Sarah knew she needed a new strategy to avoid burnout and continue growing her business.

The Solution

1. Time-Blocking for Efficiency

Sarah began by implementing time-blocking techniques. She created a detailed weekly schedule that allocated specific blocks of time to her paramedic shifts, client consultations, training sessions, and administrative work. For example:

- **Morning hours** (before her paramedic shift): Focused on business planning, responding to emails, and creating training content.

- **Weekends**: Reserved for client training sessions.

- **Evenings**: Dedicated to marketing and networking efforts.

By breaking her week into manageable chunks, Sarah found that she could prioritize her business without neglecting her paramedic responsibilities.

2. Outsourcing Administrative Tasks

Sarah realized she was spending too much time on repetitive administrative tasks. She hired a virtual assistant to manage scheduling, invoicing, and email communication. This decision freed up hours each week, allowing her to focus on client relationships and delivering high-quality training.

3. Leveraging Technology

Sarah invested in an online booking system that allowed clients to schedule training sessions directly through her website. The system synced with her calendar, reducing back-and-forth communication and ensuring her schedule stayed organized.

4. Building a Strong Network

Sarah joined local business networking groups and attended industry events to build relationships with potential clients. Over time, her network became a significant source of referrals, helping her grow her client base organically.

The Outcome

Within two years, Sarah's consulting firm had grown to serve over fifty clients, ranging from small businesses to regional corporations. The revenue generated by her business allowed her to transition to part-time paramedic work, giving her more time to focus on expanding her services. By outsourcing tasks, streamlining operations, and leveraging her network, Sarah not only avoided burnout but also achieved a sustainable balance between her career and entrepreneurship.

Chapter Thoughts

Resilience isn't just about surviving challenges; it's about thriving because of them. As a first responder turned entrepreneur, your ability to adapt, problem-solve, and lead under pressure gives you a unique edge. By embracing challenges as opportunities and implementing these strategies, you can overcome obstacles and build a business that stands the test of time.

In the next chapter, we'll explore scaling your business, focusing on expanding operations, reaching new markets, and ensuring sustainable growth. Let's keep moving forward with confidence.

CHAPTER 10

Scaling Your Business—Growing Beyond the Startup Phase

Scaling your business is about achieving sustainable growth that balances increased revenue with optimized costs and operations. As a first responder, you're already adept at managing complex situations and solving problems under pressure. These skills are invaluable as you take your business to the next level. Scaling requires foresight, discipline, and strategic planning to ensure growth doesn't compromise the quality or values that define your success.

This chapter will help you understand the strategies, considerations, and real-world examples to help guide you through the exciting yet challenging process of scaling your business.

What Does It Mean to Scale a Business?

Scaling is distinct from growth. While growth typically involves increasing revenue and expenses proportionally, scaling focuses on maximizing efficiency to increase revenue without a corresponding rise in costs. It's about doing more with less, serving more customers, expanding into new markets, or increasing profitability while maintaining operational excellence.

For example:

- A growing business might hire more employees to handle increasing workloads.

- A scaling business would instead implement automation or streamlined workflows, allowing the same team to achieve greater output without additional headcount.

The ultimate goal of scaling is to expand capacity and capability while maintaining or improving profit margins.

Signs Your Business Is Ready to Scale

Scaling too early can lead to financial strain, operational inefficiencies, or even burnout. Conversely, waiting too long can mean missed opportunities. Here are some indicators that your business is primed for scaling:

1. Consistent Revenue Growth

Your business has achieved steady and predictable revenue over a sustained period, indicating that you've found a stable market fit and demand for your product or service.

2. Excess Customer Demand

Excess customer demand is a good problem to have, but it's also a signal that your business may be ready to scale. If you're turning away customers or operating at full capacity, it's time to evaluate how you can meet growing demand without compromising the quality of your product or service.

In my business, some of our paramedic programs developed waitlists exceeding a year. This situation prompted a critical team discussion about whether and how to scale our operations. I gathered our team and started with a few fundamental questions:

1. **"Who do we serve?"**: This wasn't just about identifying our customer base, it was about reaffirming our mission. We asked ourselves whether scaling our programs to accommodate more students would align with our core purpose. We knew our program delivered outstanding results, with excellent pass rates on certification exams. Beyond just meeting demand, we recognized that expanding our capacity could significantly impact our students' careers and, by extension, the quality of care they'd provide to their future patients.

2. **"Can we maintain quality?"**: Scaling often comes with the risk of diluting quality. We knew our reputation was built on delivering high-caliber education, and any decision to expand had to preserve that standard. After careful analysis, we were confident we could uphold our quality while serving a larger student base by leveraging strategic hiring, refining operational processes, and utilizing technology to streamline learning delivery.

Scaling isn't just about increasing numbers; it's about ensuring that the essence of what made your business successful remains intact. For us, it meant expanding in a way that honored our commitment to high-quality education and impactful outcomes for both students and the communities they would serve.

If you find yourself in a similar position, ask yourself these guiding questions:

- Is there a strategic way to grow while staying true to your mission?
- What systems, staff, or technology will you need to scale effectively?
- Can you ensure that growth enhances your customer experience rather than diminishing it?

When approached thoughtfully, scaling to meet demand is not just an opportunity for growth, it's a chance to amplify your impact and serve your audience in expanded ways.

3. Proven Product or Service

Your offering has been refined, tested, and validated by the market, consistently delivering value to your customers.

4. Operational Efficiency

Your internal processes are streamlined, documented, and reliable, ensuring that your operations can handle increased demand without breaking down.

5. Financial Stability

Your business has stable cash flow, manageable debt, and a financial buffer to support the investments required for scaling.

6. Team Capacity

Scaling a business isn't just about increasing revenue or expanding services, it's about ensuring that your team has the capacity to sustain that growth. I've said many times at our school, "If we don't put people in place to manage growth, we will fail." Your ability to scale successfully depends on having a strong team that can handle increased workloads while maintaining the quality and efficiency your customers expect.

Balancing Growth with Hiring

Many business owners wrestle with the classic dilemma: *Do I hire before revenue justifies it, or do I push my current team to their limits until we can afford more staff?* The truth lies somewhere in the middle. Growth often brings periods where your existing team must stretch beyond their usual workload. However, sustained overload leads to burnout, inefficiency, and, ultimately, failure.

The key is communication and strategic planning. Your team is more likely to buy into the mission and push through the demanding periods if they understand the bigger picture: that the extra workload is temporary and that new positions will soon be added. Clarity breeds commitment. Employees need to know the plan:

- What is the roadmap for handling growth?
- When will new hires be brought in?
- How will their workload shift as the business expands?

If they see a thoughtful, strategic plan, they'll be more willing to step up during those high-growth phases. They'll also understand that it's temporary, which will help them get through the sprint, knowing it's not meant to be a prolonged effort.

Leading from the Front

Your team will always be watching what you do, not just what you say. If you expect them to work harder during an intense growth phase, they need to see that you are willing to be in the trenches with them.

At multiple points in our school's growth, I have jumped in wherever needed, whether it was answering phones, teaching a class, taking out the trash, or helping a struggling student. Nothing should be beneath the leader. If your team sees that you are willing to grind alongside them, their respect and willingness to go the extra mile will increase tenfold.

Unfortunately, I've also seen business owners who take the opposite approach, barking orders from the sidelines without lifting a finger to help. That's not leadership—that's dictatorship. People don't follow titles—they follow leaders who serve.

Knowing When to Step in and When to Step Back

As a business owner, there's a balance between being present with your team and fulfilling your role as the CEO. You must prioritize strategic leadership, focusing on growth planning, partnerships, financial management, and overall business direction. However, that doesn't mean detachment from your team's day-to-day struggles.

I relate this directly to my career in the fire service. As an incident commander, my primary role at a fire scene is strategic oversight, making sure crews are assigned properly, the incident is under control, and safety is maintained. I'm not the one advancing a hoseline or forcing entry into the building anymore. But when the fire is out, and it's time to clean up, I'll jump in to help pack hose and make sure my team is ready for the next call.

The same applies in business. Your job as a CEO is to guide the vision and strategy, but once those responsibilities are handled, **there is always an opportunity to help the team**. This mindset fosters loyalty, strengthens company culture, and ensures that your business grows with a team that is fully bought into the mission.

Build with People, Not Just Systems

As you scale, remember that your team is your greatest asset. Processes, marketing strategies, and financial models all matter, but people are what truly sustain growth. Invest in your team, communicate openly, and lead from the front. If you do this, you'll build not just a bigger business, but one that people are proud to be a part of.

Strategies for Scaling Your Business

Scaling requires a strategic approach that balances growth with sustainability. The following are key strategies to help you scale effectively.

Operational efficiency is the foundation of scalable growth. Without it, increased demand can quickly lead to bottlenecks, frustrated customers, and an overworked team, all of which can stall momentum instead of fueling expansion. The key to true scalability isn't just working harder; it's working smarter by refining processes, eliminating inefficiencies, and leveraging technology.

At our company, our COO plays a critical role in evaluating every area of our operations to identify where we can improve efficiency, ensuring that we're not just growing, but scaling. This distinction is important. Growth means getting bigger; scaling means getting bigger while becoming more efficient.

The Challenge of Change

One of the biggest challenges in optimizing operations is changing long-standing processes. The systems and workflows that got you to a certain level of success may no longer be the best fit as you grow. The problem? People get comfortable with what they know.

I've seen this firsthand. Some of our most ingrained operational processes had been in place for years. They worked—until they didn't. As we pushed for scalability, we realized that what had once been effective was now limiting our potential.

But the real challenge wasn't just identifying these inefficiencies; it was getting the team to buy into the need for change. Even with a clear vision, people don't always see the long-term benefits of change immediately. Discomfort and resistance can emerge, especially when employees feel that their established workflows are being disrupted. And here's the truth: you can articulate the vision perfectly, and they still might not get it, at least not at first.

Overcoming Resistance and Creating Buy-In

1. Involve Your Team in the Process
Instead of dictating changes, engage your team in the conversation. Ask them what's working, what's not, and where they see inefficiencies. When people feel heard, they're more likely to embrace new ideas.

2. Show, Don't Just Tell
Words alone won't always convince people. Demonstrate the impact of inefficiencies by sharing data (why we need to change), case studies, or real-life examples of how streamlining operations will improve their workload and allow us to move forward to serve a larger customer base.

3. Implement Gradual Changes

People don't resist change as much as they resist being changed. When possible, introduce adjustments in phases, allowing time for adaptation and feedback before rolling out a complete overhaul. That being said, there will be times in your business when time is of the essence. You may have waited too long to make changes, and your team is behind the curve and struggling. You need to scale, and the only way to do so is to move quickly with purpose. That change is going to be very uncomfortable for some people on your team.

4. Celebrate Quick Wins

Find small victories early in the process, whether it's cutting administrative time in half, improving turnaround times, or reducing customer complaints. Quick wins build momentum and help skeptics see the benefits of optimization.

5. Reinforce the Vision Continuously

One conversation about why you're changing things isn't enough. Keep the vision front and center. Regularly communicate how these operational improvements are moving the company toward scalability and long-term success.

Scaling requires more than just increasing revenue. It demands streamlining processes, improving efficiency, and ensuring your team is aligned with the vision. The companies that fail to optimize often hit a wall, overwhelmed by the very growth they worked so hard to achieve. But those who embrace efficiency and adaptability set themselves up for sustainable success.

Document Processes: Build Your "French Fry Playbook"

Creating standard operating procedures (SOPs) for all critical tasks is a cornerstone of scaling your business effectively. These documents act as a playbook, ensuring that as your team grows, everyone follows the same proven methods, maintaining consistency and quality across the board.

In our organization, I've referred to this as our "How to Make the French Fries" manual, a concept inspired by the legendary approach to scaling the fast-food chain McDonald's. McDonald's achieved global success not just by selling fast food but by perfecting their processes. Whether you visit a McDonald's in Boston or Los Angeles, the fries are made the same way, delivering a consistent experience to customers no matter the location.

This level of consistency didn't happen by chance. It's the result of meticulously documented processes that outline every detail of how their products are prepared, from the ingredients used to the exact cooking times, temperatures, the amount of salt they use, and how long they can sit under the heat lamp. This precision ensures that every team member, regardless of experience, can follow the same steps to achieve the same results.

Here's how to create your own "French Fry Playbook":

1. **Identify Key Processes:** Start by listing the tasks or functions critical to your business. These might include onboarding new clients, fulfilling customer orders, managing inventory, or delivering your core product or service.

2. **Break It Down into Steps:** For each process, break it down into clear, actionable steps. Use simple, straightforward language that anyone can understand, regardless of their experience level. Avoid jargon and ambiguity.

3. **Test and Refine:** Have someone unfamiliar with the task follow your SOP to see if it works as intended. If they hit any roadblocks or have questions, refine the instructions until they're foolproof. There is a great video on YouTube, "Exact Instructions Challenge - THIS is why my kids hate me. | Josh Darnit." This is a video of a dad asking his kids to provide step-by-step instructions on how to make a peanut butter and jelly sandwich. It's very amusing, but it does show how we make assumptions about what other people will know about how to accomplish a task.

4. **Incorporate Visuals:** Wherever possible, include images, diagrams, or videos to illustrate steps. Visual aids enhance clarity and make the SOPs easier to follow. In my business, I would do screen recordings to create task training videos to show new folks how to complete tasks. I remember trying to show a team member how to use a new online program we had at our school. It went something like: "Hey John, here is how you do this in our new system." I then clicked on several things, moved to different parts of the program, and then repeated it. Basically, "*Click, click, click, click.* Got that?" Of course, there was no way he could retain all that information after just one quick demonstration, especially without using the mouse himself! I soon realized that approach wasn't effective. Now, I rely on screen recordings to train new staff, giving them a reference they can revisit as often as they need.

5. **Standardize Formatting:** Ensure all your SOPs follow a consistent format, making them professional and easy to navigate. Use headings, bullet points, and numbered lists to organize information logically.

6. **Make It Accessible:** Store your SOPs in a centralized location, such as a shared drive or team management software, where your

team can easily access them. When I was the training captain for my fire department, I pitched a knowledge management system to my chief as a central repository for our standard operating procedures (SOPs). Before implementing it, we relied on two three-inch binders kept in the shift commander's office, meaning no one else had direct access to our policies and procedures without consulting the shift commander. It's remarkable to think about now, given that we digitized our SOPs and made them accessible online to every firefighter in the organization. SOPs should guide your behavior and inform your decisions based on established policies.

7. **Review and Update Regularly:** Business processes evolve over time, so it's essential to review and update your SOPs regularly to ensure they remain accurate and relevant.

The "French Fry Playbook" isn't just about documenting tasks, it's about creating a foundation for scalability. With SOPs in place, your business can grow without sacrificing quality or consistency, and new team members can hit the ground running with a clear understanding of how to execute their roles effectively. This level of preparation and clarity is what transforms a good business into a great one.

- **Adopt Automation:** Invest in tools that automate repetitive tasks, such as invoicing, email marketing, and customer support. Platforms like HubSpot, QuickBooks, and Zapier can save time and reduce errors.

- **Evaluate Technology:** Ensure your technology infrastructure, such as software, communication tools, and inventory systems, can scale with your business.

- **Eliminate Inefficiencies:** Conduct a thorough review of your operations to identify and address inefficiencies. This might involve streamlining workflows, renegotiating supplier contracts, or reallocating resources.

2. Building a Scalable Team

A strong, capable team is essential for scaling your business. As a first responder, you already understand the value of trust, leadership, and collaboration, qualities that are equally vital in a business team.

- **Hire for Growth:** Focus on roles that directly impact scaling, such as sales, marketing, or operations. Look for candidates with the skills and experience needed to support your long-term goals and fit your culture.

- **Train and Develop:** As your business grows, investing in training and development is not just an option; it's a necessity. A well-trained team is the backbone of a successful operation, especially when your business involves critical skills or high-stakes responsibilities. By equipping your employees to adapt to new challenges and take on evolving responsibilities, you can ensure consistency, quality, and resilience as your organization scales.

In my business of EMS education, training has been a cornerstone of our success. We have invested heavily in the development of our team, particularly our educators, to maintain the highest standards of teaching. When training EMTs and paramedics, consistency is paramount. Our students rely on us not only to provide the knowledge they need but to equip them with the practical skills that will save lives in their future roles. This responsibility demands a rigorous, standardized approach to education, ensuring every student receives the same high-quality instruction, regardless of the educator or course location.

But training isn't just about maintaining consistency; it's about fostering growth and innovation within your team. As businesses evolve, so do the skills required to meet new challenges. Providing your team with ongoing development opportunities, whether through workshops, certifications, or mentorship, empowers them to rise to these challenges and contribute to the organization in meaningful ways. It also boosts morale and employee engagement, creating a culture where people feel valued and invested in their own growth.

To achieve this, create a structured training program tailored to your business's needs. For example, in our EMS education business, we implement regular workshops to update instructors on new teaching methodologies, incorporate feedback from past courses, and align on standardized protocols. We also encourage peer-to-peer learning, where experienced educators mentor newer team members, fostering collaboration and a shared commitment to excellence.

Training and development should be seen as a long-term investment, not an expense. The returns are clear: a more skilled, confident, and adaptable team, improved customer satisfaction, and a stronger foundation for scaling your business. When you prioritize the growth of your team, you're not only enhancing your organization's capabilities but also building a culture of learning and excellence that will carry your business into the future.

- **Delegate Effectively:** Empower your team by delegating tasks and trusting them to execute. Micromanaging hinders productivity and growth.

- **Leverage Outsourcing:** Outsourcing specialized tasks such as graphic design, IT support, or content creation can bring in the expertise you need without the financial commitment of hiring full-time employees. In our business, outsourcing has proven to be a game-changer, giving us access to the work of highly skilled professionals while saving both time and money. By partnering with external organizations that excel in specific areas, we've been able to achieve results more quickly and efficiently. Outsourcing not only boosts productivity but also frees up internal resources to focus on core business operations, driving overall growth and success.

3. Diversifying Revenue Streams

Expanding your revenue streams reduces risk and increases income potential. Diversification allows you to reach new customer segments and tap into additional markets.

- **Complementary Products or Services:** Introduce offerings that align with your core business. For example, a fitness coach might add nutritional consulting or merchandise sales.

- **Subscription Models:** Create recurring revenue through subscription services, such as monthly memberships or ongoing support packages.

- **Digital Products:** Monetize your expertise by selling online courses, ebooks, or templates.

4. Expanding into New Markets

Reaching new customer segments or expanding into new geographic areas can dramatically increase your business's visibility, impact, and revenue—but it's not a move to be made lightly. These types of growth strategies carry both high reward and high risk, and they require intentional planning backed by market research, operational readiness, and a long-term mindset.

| Geographic Expansion

Expanding into new cities, regions, or countries may seem like the next logical step once your business is stable in your local area. However, each new geographic region presents a unique ecosystem that must be thoroughly understood. Before you expand, research is essential. You'll need to examine:

- **Regulatory Requirements**: Does the new location require special permits, licensing, insurance, or taxation practices? This is especially relevant if you're in a heavily regulated industry like health, safety, or firearms.

- **Cultural Norms and Customer Expectations**: What works in your hometown might not translate to another part of the country or even the world. Language, buying habits, and customer values can differ widely. Understanding these differences is key to offering products and services that resonate.

- **Logistical Infrastructure**: Can you fulfill orders, deliver services, or staff operations in a new area without compromising quality or increasing costs beyond what your business can support?

Many businesses begin with a test market, a new region where they can pilot a limited rollout to evaluate traction, collect feedback, and fine-tune their offerings before going all in. This phased approach can reduce risk while still offering valuable insights into potential success. I like to protect the downside whenever I can in my business. Testing makes sense and protects against the downside of a large investment that may not work.

Market Segmentation

Another powerful growth strategy is to go deeper into the market you're already in by identifying untapped or underserved customer segments. Market segmentation involves dividing your potential customer base into distinct groups based on shared characteristics, such as profession, age, lifestyle, income level, or purchasing behavior. Next you tailor your products, services, or messaging to suit their specific needs.

For example, let's say you run a safety training business geared toward fire departments. By studying your market, you may realize there's a growing demand among schools, corporate offices, or churches for similar services tailored to their environments. Adjusting your offerings slightly to serve these new groups could open up entirely new revenue streams without requiring a full geographic move.

To explore this further:

- Conduct customer interviews or surveys to identify unmet needs.

- Analyze competitor offerings to find market gaps. (This is one of my favorites, as you use your first responder advantage, because we see the world through a different lens than most people. We are just different because of our experiences during emergent events.)

- Use tools like Google Trends, industry reports, or customer data analytics to guide your segmentation strategy.

Strategic Partnerships

One of the fastest and most efficient ways to break into a new market, geographic or demographic, is through strategic partnerships. Partnering with businesses that already have credibility and reach within the market you're targeting can fast-track your growth while lowering your risk.

For instance:

- If you're expanding into a new city, partner with a local business to offer bundled services.

- If you're launching a product that serves a niche audience, collaborate with influencers or trusted figures in that space.

- If your business offers a training component, align with professional associations or schools that already serve your target market.

Strategic partnerships can also help with distribution, marketing, and operations, giving you a foothold in unfamiliar territory without having to start from scratch.

Remember, growth is not just about selling more, it's about building a business that can adapt, scale, and deliver value in new environments. Expand with purpose, and your impact can stretch far beyond what you initially imagined.

5. Leveraging Data-Driven Marketing

Scaling requires a focused marketing strategy to reach a broader audience while maintaining cost-effectiveness.

- **Invest in Digital Marketing:** Use social media advertising, email campaigns, and search engine optimization (SEO) to attract and retain customers. We invested significant capital in our website. We knew many of our students were finding us by word of mouth from past students, but about fifteen percent of our clients were finding us through online search engines. We focused our marketing on ensuring we had a solid SEO plan, and our plan would drive traffic to our website. We hired Agency Boon, a great organization that was able to recreate our website, optimize our SEO plan, and push us to many first-position keyword searches in our market space.

- **Analyze Customer Behavior:** Use analytics tools to track customer behavior, preferences, and purchasing patterns. This data helps refine your marketing strategies and offerings.

- **Focus on Customer Retention:** Retaining existing customers is more cost-effective than acquiring new ones. Implement loyalty programs, offer personalized experiences, and maintain excellent customer service.

When we set out to scale NMETC, our goal was clear: to expand our reach while staying true to our mission of providing high-quality EMS education. The challenge was to achieve growth without diluting the personal touch and student-centered approach that had become our hallmark. Scaling required a focused marketing strategy that could amplify our presence, engage prospective students, and foster loyalty among our existing ones, all while maintaining cost-effectiveness.

Avoiding Pitfalls During Scaling

Scaling can be complex and fraught with challenges. Here's how to avoid common mistakes:

Overextending Finances: Scaling a business is exciting, but it comes with financial complexities that need careful navigation. One of the most crucial aspects of scaling is ensuring your financial projections are realistic and that you have a clear plan to maintain profitability as you grow.

In my business, I quickly realized that growth didn't automatically translate to increased profit margins. At first, it seemed self-evident that more students meant more revenue, and more revenue should equal higher profits. However, as we scaled, it became clear that supporting growth required significant financial investment in personnel, infrastructure, and systems.

For example, as enrollment increased, we needed to expand our team to handle the additional workload. This included hiring more educators, administrative staff, and support personnel to maintain the quality of our programs and the level of service our students expected. We also needed to invest in infrastructure, larger facilities, advanced technology, and new equipment to accommodate the growing number of students. These expenses meant that while revenue grew, our profit margins initially tightened as we funneled resources into managing and supporting that growth.

The lesson here is that successful scaling isn't about pushing your existing team harder or stretching your resources thinner. It's about building a foundation that can sustain and manage the growth. This requires foresight, planning, and a willingness to reinvest in the business. You need to ask yourself: *What additional resources, both human and material, are needed to handle the increased demand without sacrificing quality or efficiency?*

Scaling is a delicate balance. It requires investing strategically in areas that drive long-term growth while carefully managing expenses to ensure the business remains financially healthy. By taking a thoughtful approach and avoiding the temptation to overextend your finances, you can position your business for sustainable success.

Case Studies: Lessons from Successful Scaling

Scaling a business isn't just about increasing revenue; it's about creating sustainable systems that support growth while maintaining quality. Here is an example of how one first responder successfully scaled a business, along with a breakdown of the strategies that made growth possible.

Case Study: Colin's Journey from EMT to Firearms Entrepreneur

Colin, a former EMT, had always been passionate about firearms and the industry surrounding them. After years of serving as a first responder, he decided to explore a business that aligned with his personal interests and expertise—opening a gun sales and transfer business. Like many first responders turned entrepreneurs, he started small, working within the constraints of his local regulations while slowly building his reputation.

Starting Small: The Power of a Niche Market

Colin's entry into the firearms business was modest. He secured a shared space with other gun businesses, allowing him to keep overhead costs low while gaining experience in the industry. His primary customers were friends, colleagues in the first responder community, and local firearms enthusiasts who trusted him for gun transfers and sales. Word of mouth helped drive traffic, and he built a strong foundation of repeat customers.

However, as he became more involved in the industry, Colin quickly realized that state regulations were limiting his ability to scale. He faced increasing red tape, compliance costs, and restrictions that stifled the growth potential of his business. Instead of allowing these limitations to hold him back, Colin made a bold decision: he would relocate his business to a more firearms-friendly state where he could operate without restrictions.

Making the Move: Expanding in a Business-Friendly Environment

Relocating a business is never easy, but Colin knew that moving to a state with fewer regulatory barriers would open new doors for growth. He carefully researched locations that had strong firearm markets, fewer restrictions, and business-friendly tax policies. Once he identified the right state, he opened a dedicated retail space that was designed to meet the growing needs of his customers.

By moving, he gained the ability to expand his inventory, operate with fewer legal hurdles, and serve a broader clientele. This decision proved to be a game-changer for his business.

Diversifying Revenue Streams: Beyond Firearm Sales

Rather than relying solely on direct gun sales, Colin strategically expanded his offerings to maximize profitability:

- **Ammunition Sales:** Recognizing that ammunition sales were a recurring need for his customers, he began stocking a variety of popular calibers. This addition provided a steady revenue stream and attracted more foot traffic to his retail location.

- **Consignment Services:** Colin realized that many firearm owners were looking to sell guns but didn't want to deal with the hassle of finding buyers or navigating legal transfer requirements. He introduced a gun consignment program, taking a percentage of the sale price in exchange for handling the transaction. This allowed him to generate profit without the risk of purchasing and holding excessive inventory.

- **Online Market Expansion:** As he learned more about the business, Colin recognized the potential of e-commerce. Instead of keeping a costly and extensive inventory, he optimized his website for search engine optimization (SEO) to attract buyers beyond his local community. He then developed a marketplace that drop-shipped firearms and accessories directly from his distributors. This strategy allowed him to offer a vast selection of products without the burden of maintaining a massive inventory.

By integrating e-commerce with his physical store, he was able to increase sales and efficiency while minimizing overhead costs.

Scaling Up: The Need for a Team

Colin's business growth has reached a tipping point. He's handling more customers than ever, managing both retail and online sales, and running a successful consignment program. However, with increased demand comes increased responsibility, and he recognizes that to sustain and scale his business, he needs to build a reliable team.

He's currently evaluating the key positions required to streamline operations, and is considering hiring:

- A **Sales Associate** to assist customers in-store and manage gun transfers.

- An **E-commerce Manager** to handle online orders, SEO strategy, and website updates.

- An **Inventory and Compliance Specialist** to ensure legal requirements are met and inventory is well-managed.

Colin understands that hiring strategically is crucial. His team will be a reflection of his business, and customer trust is paramount in the firearms industry.

KEY TAKEAWAYS FROM COLIN'S SUCCESS

1. **Adaptability is Key:** Colin didn't allow state regulations to stifle his growth—he moved his business to an environment where he could thrive.

2. **Diversification Increases Stability:** By expanding into ammunition sales, consignment services, and e-commerce, he created multiple revenue streams to support long-term sustainability.

3. **Technology Creates Leverage:** Optimizing his website for SEO and using a drop-shipping model allowed Colin to expand his business without excessive inventory costs.

4. **Scaling Requires a Team:** As his business grows, Colin understands that delegation is necessary to continue expansion without burning out.

Colin's journey from EMT to successful firearms entrepreneur is a testament to the power of strategic decision-making, adaptability, and leveraging multiple revenue streams to create a thriving business. With a solid foundation in place and plans for a growing team, Colin is well on his way to building a firearms business that stands the test of time.

Chapter Thoughts

Scaling your business is an exciting milestone, but it requires careful planning and execution. By streamlining operations, building a strong team, diversifying revenue streams, and strategically entering new markets, you can grow sustainably while maintaining the values and quality that set your business apart.

In the next chapter, we'll explore how to build a lasting legacy, creating a business that thrives today and continues to make an impact for years to come.

CHAPTER 11

Sustaining Success–Long-Term Strategies and Legacy Building

Your entrepreneurial journey, much like your career as a first responder, has been driven by perseverance, adaptability, and a commitment to impact. As you navigate the challenges of maintaining your business's momentum, the next phase is about ensuring its sustainability, relevance, and enduring legacy. This chapter explores strategies for fostering long-term success and building something meaningful that stands the test of time.

Sustaining success is not simply about maintaining financial stability; it requires aligning your purpose with strategies for growth, innovation, and resilience. This chapter explores Simon Sinek's concepts of **finite and infinite mindsets** and provides actionable strategies for sustaining success while preserving the values that have guided your entrepreneurial journey.

The Finite vs. Infinite Mindsets: Setting the Foundation

In *The Infinite Game*, Simon Sinek presents two contrasting approaches to business: finite and infinite mindsets. These paradigms influence how leaders define success, make decisions, and prepare for the future. Understanding these mindsets is critical as you plan for your business's long-term trajectory.

The Finite Mindset

A finite business operates with defined rules, clear competitors, and measurable goals. The focus is often on reaching a specific milestone or achieving an exit strategy, such as selling the company or achieving market dominance. Characteristics of a finite mindset include:

- **Goal-Centric Leadership:** Success is measured by revenue targets, market share, or a predetermined endpoint.

- **Exit Strategies:** Leaders plan for transitions, such as selling the business, merging, or passing it to a successor.

- **Value Optimization:** Efforts focus on maximizing the company's appeal to potential buyers or investors.

While this approach offers clarity and measurable achievements, it often lacks the adaptability required for long-term sustainability. The business's direction may also shift significantly under new leadership after the visionary exits the business.

The Infinite Mindset

In contrast, an infinite business thrives on adaptability, innovation, and impact. Leaders with an infinite mindset prioritize long-term goals, continuous growth, and resilience over immediate wins. Characteristics include:

- **Sustainability over Profitability:** The focus is on creating enduring value for customers, employees, and communities.

- **Values-Driven Leadership:** Decisions are aligned with the company's mission and vision.

- **Legacy Building:** Success is measured by the business's ability to adapt, evolve, and create positive change over time.

Infinite-mindset businesses thrive by embracing uncertainty, fostering innovation, and maintaining a strong sense of purpose. This approach aligns particularly well with first responders, whose careers are built on resilience, adaptability, and service.

At our school, money has never been the driving force. Our mission is pure, and our core values remain steadfast. The very reason we exist is summed up in our guiding principle: **NMETC exists to educate and train EMTs and paramedics so that future lives may be saved.** This purpose is not just a statement—it's the foundation of everything we do.

Our students go on to make a profound difference in the lives of their patients and the communities they serve. I often remind our staff of the immense ripple effect their work creates. Through their dedication to teaching and mentoring, their impact extends far beyond what any of us could achieve individually. Each student they train carries forward the knowledge, skills, and compassion imparted to them, magnifying our collective mission to save lives and serve others.

Our focus has always been on making a meaningful difference. The work we do is not measured in dollars but in the lives touched and the communities strengthened by the EMTs and paramedics we prepare for this vital calling. It's this legacy of service and excellence that drives us every day.

Choosing Your Path: Finite or Infinite?

As a first responder turned entrepreneur, you have a unique perspective on service, leadership, and adaptability. The choice of a finite vs. infinite mindset depends on your goals, values, and vision for the future.

The Finite Approach: Building to Exit

A **finite mindset** in business means you are working toward a clearly defined endgame. You may want to sell your company, transition it to a family member, or reach a certain milestone before moving on to something new. This model is ideal for those who see entrepreneurship as a chapter in their life, not the whole book.

Here are key strategies for building a business with a finite goal:

1. **Define Clear Goals:** Just like writing an incident action plan to handle an emergency—say, at a fire scene—building a finite business starts with establishing specific, measurable objectives. These might include revenue targets, profit margins, market share, or customer growth metrics. Know exactly what success looks like and build systems to measure progress along the way.

2. **Develop an Exit Strategy Early:** Waiting until you're ready to leave is too late. Whether you're planning a sale, merger, or internal succession, your exit strategy should guide how you structure your operations, hire your leadership team, and even price your services. Think about who might take over and what they would need to succeed without you.

3. **Maximize Value Over Time:** Focus on building a business that is efficient, well-documented, and scalable. Clean financials,

streamlined operations, and a solid customer base will increase your company's valuation and appeal to potential buyers or successors. This means optimizing your tech programs, creating SOPs, and developing a strong brand and marketing engine that doesn't rely solely on your personal efforts.

4. **Prepare for the Emotional Transition:** Letting go of something you've built can be emotionally complex. You're not just handing off a business, you're stepping away from a major part of your identity. Prepare yourself and your team for the handoff and recognize that your leadership has laid the foundation for what comes next. Give yourself permission to feel that shift and begin exploring new goals or ventures that align with your values. I liken this to retirement from your public safety job. You have to find a purpose and *what's next* in your life.

The Infinite Approach: Building to Last

On the other hand, an infinite mindset sees your business not as a vehicle to a destination but as a living, breathing legacy. You're not just trying to hit quarterly goals, you're building something that outlasts you. This path is grounded in vision, values, and a commitment to continuous evolution.

If your business is rooted in mission, perhaps improving EMS education, transforming community safety, or supporting other first responders, this approach might resonate more deeply with you and your innate need to serve.

Here's how to thrive with an infinite mindset:

1. Commit to Continuous Growth

Infinite businesses never "arrive." Instead, they evolve. This means constantly improving your products, services, and systems, fueled by curiosity and responsiveness to changing needs. It's about listening to your customers, watching the market, and having the humility to pivot when needed. Think in years and decades, not quarters.

2. Build a Values-Driven Culture

Your culture becomes your compass. When your business is built on clearly defined values, such as service, integrity, and excellence, your team knows how to act even when you're not in the room. This is crucial for long-term sustainability. Hire for alignment, reward mission-driven behavior, and use your values to guide decision-making.

3. Measure Impact Beyond Profits

Revenue keeps the lights on, but purpose keeps people inspired. In an infinite business, you measure more than money. You track:

- **Customer Satisfaction**: Are you solving meaningful problems and earning loyalty?

- **Employee Well-Being**: Are your people engaged, supported, and growing?

- **Community Engagement**: Are you contributing to the greater good?

These indicators reinforce your mission and differentiate your business in a crowded market.

4. Empower Future Leaders

A business with staying power can't depend on you forever. Start mentoring others to take on leadership roles and build succession into your DNA. Even if you never plan to leave, empowering others ensures that your impact multiplies and your mission continues even when you step back.

5. Align Everything with Vision

In an infinite business, vision isn't a statement on the wall, it's the heartbeat of your operations. Every strategy, every customer interaction, and every new initiative should tie back to your larger mission. This creates consistency, trust, and long-term loyalty from both customers and employees.

| Which Path Is Right for You?

There's no right or wrong answer here, only what's right for **you**.

Ask yourself:

- Am I building something to hand off, or something to grow with?

- Do I want the satisfaction of launching multiple ventures, or the legacy of one enduring enterprise?

- Does my current business model lend itself better to one approach over the other?

Your goals can evolve over time, and sometimes you'll move between finite and infinite strategies as your business grows. The key is to stay intentional. Whether you're laying the groundwork for an eventual exit or doubling down on long-term growth, your clarity will guide your decisions and shape your legacy.

An infinite mindset fosters a sense of purpose and resilience, ensuring your business's legacy persists long after your tenure.

Sustaining Success: Practical Strategies for Longevity

Whether you choose a finite or infinite approach, sustaining success requires thoughtful planning, consistent innovation, and a commitment to your core values. The following are key strategies to help your business thrive over the long term:

1. Define Your Vision and Purpose

Your vision is the foundation of your business's success. It provides clarity, direction, and motivation for you and your team. To define your vision:

- Reflect on your long-term goals and the legacy you want to build.
- Consider the impact you want to have on your customers, employees, and community.
- Align your vision with your personal values and the mission of your business.

A well-defined vision serves as a guiding star, ensuring that every decision and action is aligned with your ultimate purpose. For me, the story of a single mom with a dream of becoming a paramedic crystallized the vision and purpose behind creating an online education platform. She had a deep desire to serve her community at a higher level but was held back by the constraints of traditional educational approaches. Her story inspired me to think beyond the conventional, recognizing that many others like her needed a pathway to pursue their dreams while balancing the demands of life.

To serve these aspiring students, I knew I had to create something sustainable, an educational model built on a clear and purposeful foundation. That vision wasn't just about delivering content. It was about removing barriers, empowering individuals, and equipping them to make a meaningful impact in their communities. The single mom's determination became the cornerstone of our mission, reminding me that serving others and making their aspirations achievable lies at the heart of any great endeavor.

2. Foster a Culture of Innovation

Innovation is the lifeblood of long-term success. It keeps your business relevant, competitive, and adaptable. To cultivate a culture of innovation:

- Encourage creativity and risk-taking within your team.
- Stay informed about industry trends and emerging technologies.
- Regularly assess your products, services, and processes for improvement.

Innovation isn't just about introducing new ideas; it's about creating value for your customers and staying ahead of market changes.

3. Strengthen Relationships

Relationships are at the heart of any successful business. Prioritizing connections with customers, employees, and partners creates a strong foundation for growth. Key strategies include:

- **Customer Engagement:** Provide exceptional service, listen to feedback, and build trust through consistent communication.

- **Employee Development:** Invest in your team's growth, recognize their contributions, and foster a supportive work environment.

- **Partnerships:** Collaborate with other businesses and organizations that share your values and goals.

Strong relationships create loyalty, stability, and opportunities for collaboration.

4. Measure and Celebrate Impact

Success isn't just about financial metrics. Measuring and celebrating the positive impact of your business fosters a sense of purpose and accomplishment. Consider tracking:

- Customer satisfaction and retention rates.
- Employee engagement and development milestones.
- Community contributions, such as volunteer work or charitable initiatives.

Recognizing and celebrating these achievements reinforces your business's values and motivates your team to continue making a difference.

Building a Legacy: The Ultimate Measure of Success

Legacy is about creating something that endures and inspires. For first responders, legacy is deeply personal, reflecting a lifetime of service, sacrifice, and impact. Your business can extend this legacy, leaving a positive imprint on future generations.

Defining Your Legacy

To build a meaningful legacy, ask yourself:

- *What values do I want my business to embody?*
- *How can my business continue to serve and inspire others?*
- *What steps can I take today to ensure its longevity and relevance?*

Your legacy is more than the business itself; it's the culture, values, and impact you create along the way.

Creating a Legacy Framework

Building a lasting legacy for your business requires deliberate planning and purposeful action. A legacy isn't something that happens by chance— it's the result of thoughtful decisions and a commitment to ensuring your vision endures. To create a framework for your legacy, focus on three foundational areas:

1. **Succession Planning:** A thriving legacy starts with identifying and mentoring future leaders who share your vision, values, and commitment to the business's mission. Cultivate a team that understands and embraces the principles that have driven your success. Provide them with the training, guidance, and trust they need to lead effectively when the time comes for you to step back.

2. **Documenting Processes:** Standardizing and documenting your business's operations, culture, and best practices is essential for continuity. A clear playbook ensures that the systems you've built remain consistent and functional, even as leadership transitions. This includes everything from daily operations to customer interactions, so the essence of your business continues to thrive.

3. **Embedding Values:** Your core values should be the compass that guides every aspect of your business, its branding, messaging, and decision-making. When values are deeply integrated into the DNA of your organization, they resonate with employees, customers, and partners, creating a lasting impact that goes beyond profit. It is really simple: just "Do the Right Thing!"

A well-crafted legacy framework ensures that your business remains a force for good, staying true to its mission and principles long after you've stepped away. By planning intentionally and building a solid foundation, you can create something enduring that continues to make a difference in the lives of others for years to come.

| Chapter Thoughts

Sustaining success and building a lasting legacy are about more than just executing strategies. They demand a profound connection to your purpose and a relentless commitment to growth, resilience, and creating meaningful impact. As a first responder, you've already honed the ability to confront challenges, adapt to shifting circumstances, and lead with integrity under pressure. These qualities are your foundation as you step into the next chapter of your entrepreneurial journey.

Whether your path is finite, focusing on achieving specific goals and transitioning when they're met, or infinite, where your vision evolves and expands over time, your journey is a testament to service, leadership, and perseverance. By staying aligned with your values and embracing sustainability and legacy-building principles, you can create a business that thrives today while inspiring others for generations to come.

This is your legacy: a life driven by purpose, guided by impact, and defined by enduring success. Keep pushing forward, embracing the highs and learning from the lows, and never lose sight of the profound difference you can make in your business, your community, and beyond. The journey may not always be easy, but the rewards are immeasurable. Let your vision light the way, and continue building something truly extraordinary.

CHAPTER 12

Preparing for the Unknown–Ensuring Resilience in an Ever-Changing World

Entrepreneurship, like life itself, is a journey into the unknown, filled with both incredible opportunities and unexpected challenges. It's a dynamic path that demands not only innovation and vision but also the ability to adapt and persevere when things don't go as planned. As a first responder, you're no stranger to uncertainty. You've faced critical situations head-on, relying on your training, quick thinking, and composure to navigate the unpredictable nature of emergencies. These same qualities—preparation, adaptability, and resilience—are the tools for navigating the entrepreneurial landscape and ensuring your business thrives in the face of change.

This chapter isn't just about surviving challenges; it's about building a business that can bend without breaking, a business that emerges from trials stronger and more determined. We'll explore actionable strategies to cultivate resilience, not only within yourself as a leader but also within your team and the very foundation of your business. Think of resilience as the armor that protects your business from the inevitable storms, economic downturns, unexpected disruptions, and those moments that test your resolve. A resilient business isn't just built to last; it's built to evolve, adapt, and continue making a difference, no matter what comes its way.

The Strength of a Resilient Business

Imagine a tree standing tall amid a raging storm. Its branches may sway, and its leaves may rustle, but its roots hold firm, anchoring it to the ground. That's resilience in action, the ability to weather the storm and emerge stronger on the other side. In the world of business, resilience is more than just survival; it's a competitive advantage that allows you to:

- **Navigate Disruptions:** Whether it's an economic downturn, a shift in your industry, or a global crisis, a resilient business can adapt and find new paths forward.

- **Outpace Competitors:** When challenges arise, adaptable organizations can respond more quickly, seizing opportunities that others might miss.

- **Ensure Longevity:** Resilience safeguards your business's future, allowing it to overcome obstacles and maintain steady growth.

- **Inspire Confidence:** A resilient leader instills trust and loyalty in employees, customers, and stakeholders, creating a strong foundation for collective success.

Resilience Starts with the Leader

As a first responder, you've faced your share of high-pressure situations. You've learned to stay calm under pressure, focus on solutions, and make critical decisions when it matters most. These qualities are invaluable in entrepreneurship, where challenges are inevitable, and your ability to lead with resilience sets the tone for your entire team.

Think back to a time when you faced a particularly difficult call. Maybe it was a multi-vehicle accident, a raging structure fire, a robbery in progress, or a complex medical emergency. In those moments, your ability to maintain composure, assess the situation, and take decisive action was crucial, not only for the people you were helping but also for your team's morale and effectiveness.

The same principles apply in business. When the inevitable challenges arise, your ability to stay calm, focus on solutions, and project confidence can make all the difference. Remember, your team looks to you for guidance, especially during times of uncertainty. Your resilience becomes their resilience, creating a ripple effect that strengthens your entire organization.

Identifying and Managing Risks

Just as you wouldn't enter a burning building or a violent crime scene without assessing the risks, you shouldn't embark on your entrepreneurial journey without understanding the potential challenges. Risks in business come in many forms: financial, operational, competitive, or even global events beyond your control. By recognizing these vulnerabilities, you can develop proactive strategies to mitigate their impact and protect your business.

Think of risk management as your early warning system, helping you anticipate potential problems and prepare for the unexpected. It's about asking questions like:

- What are the biggest threats to our business's financial stability?
- How can we make our operations more efficient and less prone to disruptions?
- Who are our main competitors, and how can we stay ahead of the curve?

- Are there any changes in regulations or laws that could impact our business?
- How could global events like economic downturns or natural disasters affect our operations?

By proactively addressing these questions, you're protecting your business and building a foundation for long-term success.

Building Resilience into Your Business

Resilience isn't something that just happens; it's the result of intentional planning and consistent effort. It's about creating systems, processes, and a company culture that can adapt and thrive in the face of change. Here are some key areas to focus on:

- **Financial Resilience:** Maintaining strong financial health is crucial. This means keeping cash reserves, monitoring your cash flow, minimizing debt, and diversifying your income streams. Think of it as building a financial cushion to absorb unexpected shocks and maintain stability during challenging times.

- **Technological Resilience:** Technology is constantly evolving, and your business needs to keep up. Embrace automation, use data to make informed decisions, and choose scalable solutions that can grow with your business.

- **Operational Flexibility:** Streamline your processes, cross-train your employees, and build strong relationships with multiple suppliers to avoid disruptions. Consider outsourcing specialized tasks to stay agile and adapt to changing demands.

- **Building a Resilient Team:** Invest in training to keep your team's skills sharp and adaptable. Foster a culture of collaboration and open communication so everyone feels empowered to contribute to solutions.

Adapting to Change: The Key to Long-Term Success

In the ever-changing world of business, adaptability is essential. The ability to pivot, adjust your strategies, and seize new opportunities is what sets successful businesses apart. Here are some ways to cultivate adaptability:

- **Continuous Innovation:** Encourage creativity and experimentation within your team. Be open to new ideas, pilot innovative solutions on a small scale, and stay curious about industry developments and customer feedback.

- **Cultivating a Growth Mindset:** View setbacks as learning opportunities, promote flexibility within your organization, and invest in your team's development.

- **Developing Strategic Partnerships:** Collaborate with other businesses to expand your reach and offerings. Build alliances within your industry to address common challenges and engage with your community to strengthen relationships and build customer loyalty.

Building a Legacy: More Than Just Resilience

Resilience ensures your business can weather the storms, but building a legacy ensures your impact extends far beyond your own journey. It's about creating something that continues to inspire, serve, and make a difference long after you're gone.

Think about the values you want your business to embody, the positive impact you want it to have on the world, and the story you want it to tell. To build a legacy:

- **Document Your Knowledge:** Create detailed records of your processes, strategies, and the lessons you've learned along the way.

- **Mentor Future Leaders:** Share your expertise and passion to develop the next generation of leaders within your organization.

- **Embed Your Values in Your Company Culture:** Ensure that your mission and principles guide every decision and action within your business.

Forging a Legacy: From Firehouse to Foundership

Resilience helps your business endure the inevitable challenges, but legacy allows your business to live on, grow, evolve, and create a lasting impact far beyond your own direct involvement. Legacy is not just about what you build; it's about who you build along the way.

If you've served any time in the firehouse, ambulance, or on patrol, you've experienced this firsthand. Remember when a brand-new recruit walked through the station doors for the first time? Nervous. Green. Not quite sure what to expect. What happened next? A seasoned first responder took them under their wing, taught them the ropes, showed them the culture, held them accountable, and, most importantly, believed in their potential. That's how leaders are shaped in our world.

It's the same in business.

If you want your company to outlast you, you have to start thinking like a mentor, not just a founder. You have to create systems, pass down knowledge, and develop people who can one day take the lead.

Chapter Thoughts

Your experiences as a first responder have equipped you to face the unknown with courage and clarity. These same qualities will serve you well as an entrepreneur, guiding you through the inevitable uncertainties of building and running a business. By cultivating resilience, embracing adaptability, and focusing on building a legacy that matters, you're not just preparing for the unknown; you're creating a future filled with opportunity and lasting impact.

This chapter marks the culmination of your entrepreneurial journey, as outlined in this book. You've learned to identify opportunities, overcome challenges, and build a business that reflects your values and aspirations. Now, as you look ahead, embrace the uncertainty with confidence, knowing you have the tools and the mindset to not just survive but thrive.

The End of This Book, the Beginning of Your Journey

Thank you for allowing me to share with you my journey, my experiences as a first responder and an entrepreneur, the lessons I've learned, and the strategies that have helped me navigate the challenges of building a multimillion-dollar business while still doing the job I love. Writing this book has been a deeply personal reflection on the path I've walked, and it's my hope that it inspires you to believe in your ability to create something extraordinary.

The truth is that building a successful business is absolutely possible, even as you continue to serve as a first responder. I am living proof of this. You can achieve financial freedom while honoring your passion for serving your community. It won't always be easy. There will be late nights, difficult decisions, and moments of doubt. But don't give up. Keep pushing forward, even when the obstacles seem insurmountable, because the reward of creating something meaningful and lasting is worth every ounce of effort.

Acknowledgments: Gratitude for My Guides and Mentors

I would not be where I am today without the guidance, mentorship, and encouragement of those who have walked alongside me at different points on this journey. I want to take a moment to thank the incredible business coaches who have profoundly impacted my growth:

- **The Ramsey Organization**: Your principles of stewardship, financial discipline, and integrity have been a cornerstone of how I approach business and life.

- **Alex Judd at Path for Growth**: Your coaching helped me clarify my mission, focus on my impact, and develop a leadership style that inspires my team to greatness.

- **Coach Micheal Burt**: Your energy, vision, and relentless encouragement have taught me to think bigger and embrace the challenges that come with pursuing excellence.

Each of you has shaped my journey in inspiring ways, and for that, I am eternally grateful. Your influence is woven into the pages of this book, and I hope the lessons you've taught me will now reach countless others.

A Heartfelt Thank You to My Family

To my wife, Kim: None of this would have been possible without your unwavering love, patience, and support. Over the years, you've stood by me through the late nights, missed dinners, constant travel, and my relentless drive to build something meaningful. You've been my rock, my partner, and my biggest cheerleader. Thank you for always believing in me, even when the challenges seemed daunting. Our success is as much yours as it is mine.

To my children, Colin, Bridget, and Kiera: Thank you for your understanding, patience, and love over the years. I know I've missed some important milestones in your lives because I was "taking care of people," with my other family at the firehouse, or building NMETC into the organization it is today. Your willingness to share me with others in need is a testament to your own strength and generosity. Thank you for being exceptional patients in skills labs for our students at the school, and for contributing to our mission in your own unique way. I couldn't be prouder that each of you has chosen to carry on our family tradition of taking care of people by becoming EMTs yourselves. Watching you embrace this path fills me with pride and joy.

Your love and support have been the foundation of everything I've built. This book, this journey, and this success—all of it is because of you!

A Message of Encouragement

To those of you just starting out, or perhaps struggling to find your way forward, don't stop. Keep taking steps, no matter how small, toward your goals. Surround yourself with people who lift you up, who challenge you, and who see the potential in you, even when you don't see it in yourself. Remember, every great business starts with an idea, a spark of inspiration, and a willingness to take the first step.

Don't let fear hold you back. You already possess the resilience, discipline, and problem-solving skills that have made you an incredible first responder. Those same qualities will make you a successful entrepreneur. Keep learning, stay curious, and embrace the setbacks as opportunities to grow.

Your Journey, Your Legacy

This book is the culmination of my journey, a journey that has taught me how to balance my commitment to the fire service and the people I serve with my passion for building something that creates value for others. It's a journey that proves financial freedom is not just a dream but a reality that you can achieve without walking away from the work you love.

As you close this book, I want you to open a new chapter in your own life. Whether you're just starting out or already on your way, I hope you feel inspired, equipped, and empowered to take bold steps toward building your business and creating a legacy that will endure.

Thank you for reading, for dreaming big, and for believing in what's possible. I'll leave you with this thought: The journey ahead will not always be easy, but it will be worth it. Stay committed to your vision, remain steadfast in your values, and never stop pursuing the extraordinary.

From one first responder turned entrepreneur to another, I am cheering for you every step of the way.

With deep gratitude and encouragement,
Brad Newbury

THANK YOU FOR READING MY BOOK!

DOWNLOAD YOUR FREE GIFTS

Just to say thanks for buying and reading my book, I would like to connect with you, no strings attached!

Scan the QR Code:

I appreciate your interest in my book and value your feedback as it helps me improve future versions. I would appreciate it if you could leave your invaluable review on Amazon.com with your feedback. Thank you!

www.ingramcontent.com/pod-product-compliance
Lightning Source LLC
Chambersburg PA
CBHW031504180326
41458CB00044B/6689/J